LORETTA SANTINI

VESUVIUS
HERCULANEUM - POMPEII

Published and printed by

plurigraf

NARNI - TERNI

Photographs: Archivio Plurigraf
Aerial photos authorization S.M.A. n.506 del 20-6-91

© Copyright by CASA EDITRICE PLURIGRAF
S.S. Flaminia, km 90 - 05035 NARNI - TERNI - ITALIA
Tel. 0744 / 715946 - Fax 0744 / 722540 - (Italy country code: +39)
All rights reserved. No Part of this publication may be reproduced.
Printed: 1999 - PLURIGRAF S.p.A. - NARNI

66 Treacherous ground under a pure sky; ruins of unimaginable luxury, abominable and sad; seething waters; caves exhaling sulphur fumes; slag hills forbidding all living growth; barren and repulsive areas; but then, luxuriant vegetation, taking root wherever it can, soars up out of all the dead matter, encircles lakes and brooks, and extends its conquest even to the walls of an old crater by establishing there a forest of noble oaks". So Goethe, writing from Naples on 1st March 1787, describes the Neapolitan landscape, of which Vesuvius represents the fulcrum and mainspring. Formed in a depresson of the Campanian basin, between the Lattari, Sarnesi, Avellinesi and Matese mountain groups, Monte Petrella and the promontory of Gaeta, Vesuvius forms part of the chain of volcanoes distributed along the geological faults which were formed millennia ago parallel to the Appennines, along the Tyrrhenian littoral, following the sinking of the Tyrrhenid formation on the one side and the raising of the Apennines on the other. It is a volcano of enclosure-type, consisting as it does of two concentric cones, of which the external one, Monte Somma, is a volcano formed at a yet earlier period, and the interior one, Vesuvius proper, of more recent formation. As regards its geological structure, we may say that Vesuvius is a polygenic volcano, i.e. formed by numerous successive eruptions. It is mainly basalt in composition, and is a mixed volcano, formed of miscellaneous lava and detritus, ancient and more recent lava. The oldest deposits of lava in particular constitute the cone of Monte Somma, while the more recent ones mainly form the present Vesuvius. It is thought that the volcano's vent-hole reaches down to a considerable depth, right down to below the Triassic formations. Four geological ages can be distinguished, each characterized by particular types of rock. The first period starts at the beginning of the Quaternary and corresponds to the formation at the base of the volcano, consisting of trachytes and trachyte-related tufas. During the second period, between 6000 and 3000 B.C., leucitic-basaltic

rocks were formed over the base previously described. Formations of the same type continued in the third period too, between 3000 B.C. and the modern age, while the rocks of the final period - i.e. the present period - are largely of leucotefrite and vesuvite type. As for the form of the volcano before the eruption of 79 A.D., the first to be minutely described, we know very little. Some scholars, basing their theory on three ancient frescoes, one found at Herculaneum and two at Pompeii, and on what Strabo and Florus say, maintain that before this date the volcano had only one summit. Others, by contrast, affirm that it was already twin-peaked and that the eruption of 79 was confined to the inner cone. What is clear, on the other hand, is that Vesuvius presented all the appearances of an idyllic mountain in antiquity: its flanks were clad with chestnut-trees, vineyards and woodland. It was a fertile and pleasant land, dear to Bacchus and his devotees thanks to its sparkling wines: a land that had not yet experienced the terrible days of fire and destruction in the year 79 of our era. Only a few scholars in antiquity, such as Diodorus Siculus, Vitruvius and especially Strabo, who had visited Vesuvius in 19 A. D., had noted the real nature of the mountain. To Seneca, who died in 65 A. D., we owe the news of the earthquake that seriously damaged Pompeii, Herculaneum, Stabiae, Nuceria and Neopolis on 5 February of the year 62, and that may be considered the premonitory sign of the volcano's reawakening in 79. On 24 August of that year, in fact, Vesuvius suddenly awoke from its long slumber and in a terrible eruption buried Pompeii, Stabiae and Herculaneum.

While the latter was inundated and destroyed by a torrent of mud, mixed with sand and ashes, the other two cities were destroyed by a huge, dense asphyxiating cloud of ash, pumice stones and detritus. The most illustrious victim of the catastrophe was undoubtedly the Elder Pliny, naturalist and commander of the fleet of Misenum, who had immediately sailed from Misenum to bring aid to the victims and to observe the phenomenon at close hand. In a letter sent to the historian Tacitus, his

nephew the Younger Pliny gives us a detailed and precise description of that dramatic event. We quote some passages of this below, of interest for anyone about to visit Vesuvius: "On the 9th day before the calends of September (i.e. 24th August), about one in the afternoon, my mother asked him (the Elder Pliny) to observe a cloud that had suddenly appeared, and was of a very unusual size and shape. He had just returned from taking the benefit of the sun, and after bathing himself in cold water, and taking a slight repast, had retired to his study. On being told of the cloud, he asked for his shoes, and climbed up to an eminence, from whence he might more distinctly view the phenomenon. It was not at that distance discernible from what mountain this cloud issued, but it was found afterwards to ascend from Mount Vesuvius. I cannot give you a more exact description of its appearance and shape than by resembling it to that of a pine tree, for it shot up to a great height in the form of a trunk, which extended itself at the top into various branches; occasioned, I imagine, either by a sudden gust of air that impelled it, the force of which decreased as it advanced upwards, or

the cloud it left being pressed back by its own weight, expanded in this manner. It appeared sometimes white, and sometimes dark and spotted, having been impregnated with earth and cinders... Already the cinders, which grew thicker and hotter the nearer he approached, fell into the ships, together with pumice-stones and black pieces of burning rock; they were also in danger of being driven aground by the sudden retreat of the sea, and from the huge fragments which rolled down from the mountain, and obstructed all the shore... In the meanwhile the eruption from Vesuvius had ignited huge flames in many points... the roofs were shaken by frequent and violent earthquakes... people did not know whether to trust to the houses, or fly to the open fields, where the rain of ash and calcined stones, though light, yet fell in large showers, and threatened destruction". So Pliny describes the various phenomena that accompanied the eruption, which have been confirmed by modern science and by the findings of the excavations of the buried cities.

The dramatic history of the eruptions did not end there: they continued with the disastrous eruptions in 202 and 472, by which the inhabited centres which were in the process of being reconstructed over the ruins of the previous towns were presumably destroyed, and that in 512, which caused a catastrophe of such unimaginable proportions that Theoderic, King of the Goths, remitted the taxes of the stricken population. Other eruptions followed in 685, 993, 1036 and 1139. Those subsequently reported in 1306 and 1500 are

open to doubt. It seems, in fact, th[at] after the eruption of 1139, the vo[l]cano relapsed into a period of tot[al] slumber, so much so that it came t[o] be cultivated right up to its cone an[d] to have its crater covered with wood[] land. But on 16 December 1631 th[e] volcano reawoke and did so with te[r]rible consequences: the villages [at] the foot of the mountain were com[]pletely destroyed; the lava flowe[d] right down to the coast, causing th[e] death of 3,000 people; and the dar[k]ness generated by the clouds [of] steam and ashes enveloped southe[rn] Italy as far as Taranto for several day[s]. Other phases of activity ensued i[n] the course of the 17th and 18th cen[]turies, and during one of these, i[n] 1767, the lava surrounded the littl[e] church of San Vito, without de[]molishing it, was deflected toward[s] San Giorgio a Cremano, and ad[]vanced on Naples. After the erupti[on] of 1794 which destroyed Torre de[l] Greco, others followed in the cours[e] of the 19th century, culminating [in] that of 1906 which erupted with e[x]plosive force and caused conside[r]able damage, especially to the tow[ns] of Ottaviano and San Giuseppe Ves[u]viano. The present century has bee[n] marked by two other intense perio[ds] of activity, one from 1913 to 1929, an[d] the other from 1933 to 1944, aft[er] which the volcano entered a quie[s]cent phase which still continues t[o]day. Vesuvius, as we have alrea[dy] mentioned, is a twin-peaked mou[n]tain: the peak to the left is Mon[te] Somma (1132 m), the one to the rig[ht] the Vesuvian cone or Vesuvius pro[p]er (1182m). The saddle between th[e] two peaks is at an altitude of c. 700 [m]. Originally there was only one pea[k,] Monte Somma, whose cone, as lea[d]ing scholars maintain, collapsed [in] the terminal phase of the eruption [of] 79 A.D., forming an enormous shallo[w] crater, within which the cone of Ves[u]vius arose. The depression that sep[a]rates the Vesuvian cone from t[he] delicately jagged crest of Monte So[m]ma is called the Atrio del Cavallo [in] its western part and the Valle del I[n]ferno in its eastern part. The two va[l]leys as a whole form the Valle del G[i]gante.

EXCURSIONS TO VESUVIUS

The ascent of Vesuvius is a fascinati[ng] and scenic experience. The views

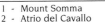

1 - Mount Somma	5 - An Old Flue
2 - Atrio del Cavallo	6 - A Recent Flue
3 - The Crater of Vesuvius	7 - A Secondary Mouth
4 - A Cone of Lapilli	8 - Lava-Flow

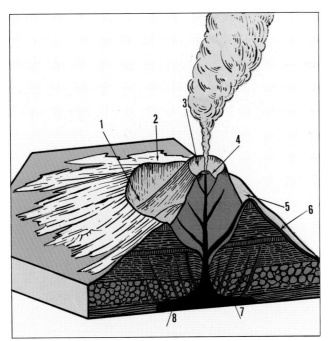

Here are other pictures referring to the last period of activity of the Vesuvius, during which the lava flowed along the area of the so called Atrio del Cavallo», for about 1270 metres from the crater, till it reached 100 metres on the sea-level. It badly damaged the cultivations and the built-up areas of S. Sebastiano and Massa, where two-thirds of the buildings were destroyed. After the lava-flow there were the so called lavic springs, which spectacularly threw the magma up to 4000 5000 metres. Then followed some explosions which were more spectacular by night and various earthquakes. During the years following the end of the paroxysm, since the brink became larger because of frequent collapses, the depth of the crater decreased.

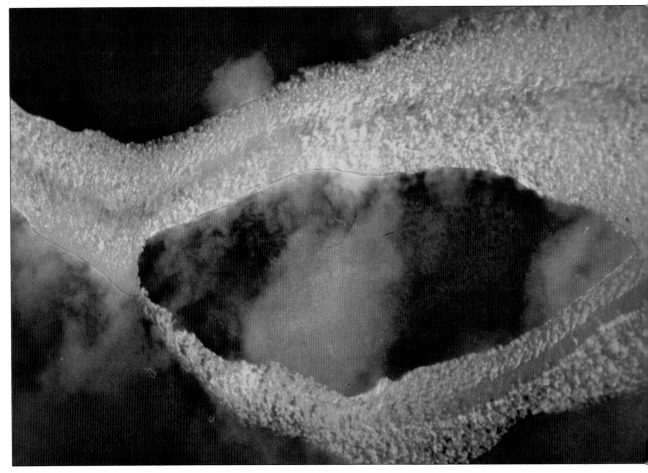

ffords are incomparable and majes-
ic, thanks both to the variety of land-
cape we pass through from the foot
f the mountain to the lip of its crater,
nd the extensiveness of the panora-
as it commands over the surround-
ng hills and towns, and over the
weeping expanses of the coastal
lain to the sea beyond. The most
onvenient and popular way of access
o Vesuvius is the road that runs from
esina, a little town of ancient origins,
n part built over the buried Hercula-
eum. Ascending through fertile vine-
ards and olive-groves, the road then
egins to climb the slopes of Vesu-
ius, covered by lava of various peri-
ds and presenting a diversity of
tructure. After passing the Piano
elle Ginestre (Plain of Broom),
amed after the humble yellow-flow-
ring shrubs hymned by Leopardi
uring his stay in Naples, we come to
he lava fields deposited by the
ruption of 1895, characterized by
ope-like formations containing large
rystals of leucite, also known as
hite garnet of Vesuvius. The road
hen winds up along the tufa slopes
f the Colle dei Canteroni, on which
tands the large building in the neo-
lassical style of the Vesuvian Obser-
atory. Crossing the Fosso della Ve-
rana and skirting the lava flows of
944 which are superimposed over
hose of 1872 and 1895-99, we reach
he Colle Umberto, from whose sum-
it magnificent views can be enjoyed
ver the Observatory below as far as
he coast. On reaching the Atrio del
Cavallo, the road bifurcates: the road
o the left, the so-called Strada Ma-
rone Occidentale, leads to the Colle
Margherita, covered by the lava and
etritus of the last eruption, and then
o the edge of the crater; the road to
he right leads to the Lower Station of
he Chairlift, which offers wonderful
anoramic views stretching from the
orrentine Peninsula to the Phle-
raean Fields and the islands in the
ulf. In a few minutes we reach the
pper Station, from where a pathway
ewn through the petrified lava, ash
nd pumice stones leads to the lip of
he crater. The Atrio del Cavallo, the
eclivity between the two peaks
overshadowed by the slopes of
Monte Somma, may also be reached
rom Boscotrecase, a large agricul-
ural centre spread out over the low-

er slopes of Vesuvius. The road from here, known as the Strada Matrone, ascends the south-eastern flank of the volcano, at first amid flourishing vineyards from whose grapes the famous "Lacryma Christi" wine is produced, then through dense woodland, and finally through the desolate landscape of lava flows. Undoubtedly more strenuous, but of great interest, are the ascents to the crater that can be made on foot, along good footpaths, departing from Torre del Greco, or Ottaviani, or Somma Vesuviano. In winter snow very often covers the flanks and crater of Vesuvius. Its top decapitated, its form deranged and altered by terrible eruptions, the volcano has been at times beneficial, at times tragically ruinous, for the towns and villages in its vicinity. The Roman poet Martial wrote in 88 A.D.: "This is Vesuvius, once green with vine-leaves; here the golden grapes had filled the vats... Now all lies buried by the flames and the terrible fire". Yet for the towns and villages scattered over the plain, round the ample base of Monte Somma, Vesuvius has always represented a source of richness, because its ashes have made the soil of this region fertile, so much so that the ancients called it Campania Felix. This land, so intensively cultivated with vegetables, potatoes, wheat, maize, hemp and walnuts, owes its extraordinary fertility to the volcanic material that constitutes its surface. In a sense, Vesuvius has been, in miniature, for Campania what the Nile has represented for Egypt. Mt. Somma has a base with a perimeter some 75 km long, round which the "circumvesuviana" railway line runs. The circumference of the crater of this earlier volcano measures some 12 km, with an average diameter of c. 3500 m.

The maximum height of this outer cone is 1132 m. at the Punta Nasone. It is believed, however, that in the past, before its top was blown off, the cone must have reached a height of 2500 m.

As for Vesuvius itself, when it was active, its crater and height varied according to the alternating phases of destruction or reconstruction. At the present time, the highest point of Vesuvius has a height of 1182 m, while its crater has a diameter of c.

700 m, roughly equivalent to a fifth of the size of the crater of Mt. Somma During our visit to the volcano, we should not forget the many splendid villas dotted over the green and gentle lower slopes of Vesuvius. They mainly date to the 18th century. Indeed the owners and guests of these villas were always strongly attracted to this area not only by the beauty of its landscape and the salubrity of its air, but also by the vicinity of the buried cities of Herculaneum and Pompeii with their priceless archaeological heritage, and by the evocativeness of scenery that seems to be so potently imbued with the spirit of the classical world. It was in these enchanting places, where the Romans had once recreated themselves, that a series of magnificent and monumental villas were built in past centuries, often by famous architects.

Almost as a counterpart to the garland of coastal villas we have briefly mentioned, a ring of picturesque little towns encircles the other side of Vesuvius, on the side of Monte Somma: Ponticelli and Pollina, Santa Anastasia, Somma and Ottaviano, ancient towns with a noble tradition which deserve to be visited, rich as they are in historical memories and in art. Of the powerful Aragonese towers of Somma only a few traces now remain.

But the Medici castle of Ottaviano is preserved intact, in its elegant 16th century lines. Standing high on the slopes of Monte Somma, it dominates the whole of the countryside below it. The artistic and historical capital of this Vesuvian hinterland is Nola, a town that has been illustrious since Roman times, and one that represents an important stage between the Christianized world of late Roman times and the more solemn world of the Byzantine and Romanesque Middle Ages.

If we climb up to the brink of the crater, the great abyss that opens up before us is one that excites both horror and fascination. The rust-red walls of the crater that plummet precipitously into the depths, where the fluid and later solidified lava has left white and grey traces; the huge gorge closed by cold, grey, irremovable blocks of detritus; the activity of the fumaroles that, by depositing sul-

phates, chlorides and other minerals, are the cause of the large yellowish blotches along the walls -all combine to form a spectacle of awesome power, and testify to the incalculable danger of the forces that the mountain encloses.

Today the volcano is in a period of quiescence. Some scientists believe that it is actually extinct. But others, who have diligently studied the activity of Vesuvius in the course of the centuries, have noted that periods of activity alternate quite regularly with periods of quiescence.

The life of the volcano is monitored and studied day after day by the Vesuvian Observatory, built by Ferdinand II in 1841-45, and designed by Gaetano Fazzini. Situated in a commanding position on the Colle dei Canteroni, the furthermost western spur of Monte Somma, the building has so far been spared from the brunt of the eruptions, even though it has been periodically struck by clouds of ash and pumice-stones, shaken by earth tremors and threatened by la-

va. Equipped with the most up-to-date apparatus, and furnished with an interesting and comprehensive collection of Vesuvian minerals and an extremely specialized library, the Observatory is a first-class scientific institution that has monitored with scrupulous attention the various eruptions, and made the most painstaking and complete study of volcanism. Apart from field research, the centre carries out meteorological, seismic and gravimetric tests, and surveys of atmospheric electricity and terrestrial magnetism.

The inside of the crater is entirely covered with the explosive products of the eruption of 1944. Many fumaroles or smoke-holes emerge from the upper walls. It was on Vesuvius that Spartacus and his followers sought refuge during the slave revolt in 73 B.C. Sent to quell the rebellion, the Roman praetor Clodius Pulcher, at the head of 3000 soldiers, occupied the only access to the mountain so as to cut off every escape route for the rebels. However, Spartacus and his

men, having managed to descend to the plain with the help of shoots cut from wild vines, took Clodius and his forces by surprise and vanquished them. Before 79 A.D. Vesuvius had been known for its excellent wines: its slopes were in fact clad by luxuriant vineyards and its peak was covered by dense woodland rich in wild game, especially wild boars. Wine amphorae from Pompeii often bear the inscription "Vesvinum" or "Vesuvinum", i.e. the wine of Vesuvius, and in the kitchens of Pompeii the head of a wild boar is often seen painted. Only a few scholars in antiquity, such as Diodorus Siculus, Strabo and notably Vitruvius had noted the volcanic nature of the mountain. Pompeii itself had been built on prehistoric lava fields and its streets had been paved using volcanic material. Yet even during the following centuries, in spite of the numerous eruptions, the slopes of the volcano were intensively cultivated right up to the summit, thanks to their particular fertility.

The Valle Dell'Inferno.
Opposite: The inside of the crater.

There are many places in Italy characterized by peculiar scenic fascination, but it is only in the disinterred cities of Pompeii and Herculaneum that we are offered a direct image of ancient Roman life. Rediscovered after 18 centuries of oblivion, they represent the most complete and most evocative expression of Campanian archaeology and the best means of gaining knowledge of ancient life. Volcanoes and earthquakes have at various times and in various places destroyed human life. But only in Pompeii and Herculaneum did it happen that a tremendous eruption laid them waste while at the same time preserving the works of man. And this has made it possible for posterity to disinter cities that had been entombed with their houses, their furnishings, their paintings, even the inscriptions scored on their walls, and so witness the most astonishing revelation of life as lived in antiquity. Fires, wars and sacks have hardly ever totally destroyed a city, but here the cataclysm was such as to mark the end, or the interruption, of every form of life in the space of a few hours or a few days. Man never returned to those ruins to restore or rebuild; he did so only with the religious feelings and human compassion aroused by exhumation.

We are able to reconstruct the drama of the catastrophe far better than the history of a siege or an assault. The letter in which Pliny the Younger described to the historian Tacitus, his great friend, the death of his maternal uncle, the Elder Pliny, who had hastened with the Roman fleet of Misenum to the scene of the eruption when the paroxysm was at its height, is not only a gem of epistolary literature, but also an invaluable volcanological witness to the various phenomena that accompanied the cataclysm. The stratification of the eruptive material forming a layer of small stones and ash five or six metres thick at Pompeii, or a confused mass of hardened mud over twelve metres thick at Herculaneum, the collapse of roofs, the traces of lighting flashes and fires, and the death from asphyxia that suddenly overcame the inhabitants during their desperate flight to thè sea, are all phenomena that can be vividly grasped from the indescribable experience of the excavations and that enable us to relive the human tragedy of the two buried cities.

According to Pliny's text and the most reliable reconstruction of the manuscript sources, the sudden eruption of Vesuvius that led to the death of the two cities occurred on 24 August in the year 79 A.D. It lasted two days, and by dawn of the third day the body of admiral Pliny lay wrapped in its shroud at Stabiae, the victim of civic duty and of his own insatiable curiosity as a naturalist.

Vesuvius had been dormant since time immemorial: vineyards and woodland covered its flanks; villas and farms were dotted over its lower slopes. The first fearsome explosion of the mountain took the inhabitants by surprise. The furious hail of small stones on roofs and terraces forced them to seek safer shelters; but the dense, viscous and whirling rain of ashes gave them no respite. It forced them to seek a way of escape through the foot-clogging mounds of ash. But by this time the air was no longer breathable. They were suffocated, and fell as they fled, on the roads, in the fields, both inside and outside the walls, bearing with them only the few personal possessions they had collected in haste before embarking on that desperate flight. Then the river of molten lava mixed with mud inexorably tightened Herculaneum in its grip, burying all its houses and completely altering its topography. In a few minutes the fate of the city was sealed. Herculaneum had been founded at the foot of Vesuvius on a terrace that formed a natural promontory on the coast, open to the sea, and almost at the centre of the great curve of the Gulf in such a way as to embrace it from the promontory of Misenum to Cape Ateneo. Built on dry and fertile volcanic soil, and fanned by cooling western beezes in summer, Herculaneum had naturally been destined to attract to its outskirts those maritime and semi-coastal villas that the Romans had a particular predilection for. It was indeed in Herculaneum that the Villa of the Papyri, the richest villa of antiquity, had been built. The lack of any extensive hinterland and the closeness of Naples itself did not permit it to develop any considerable commercial or in-

dustrial activity. But the major coastal road from Naples to Pompeii, to Nocera and the south, was routed through one of its main thoroughfares, and Herculaneum became an important transit point on the land route and of the coastal trade by sea.

In origin it was only a fortified port and vantage point of the Greeks of Cumae during their initial expansion in the Gulf. Like Pompeii, it was linked to the myth and legend of Hercules, from whom it derived its name. After the foundation of Neapolis, it was then developed as a real city by the Greeks of Naples, who gave it a plan that faithfully respected, in the geometric layout of its streets, the typical plan of a Greek city: 3 *decumani* running from east to west and 5 *cardines* running from north to south in fact intersected each other at right angles to form a chequerboard pattern of streets and to delimit the rectangular *insulae* or building blocks, though these are different in size and extent. Occupied by the Samnites and with its own independent statutes, Herculaneum became gradually drawn into the ambit of Rome. It was involved in the Social Wars, and in 80 B.C. was endowed with the Roman institutions not of a colony, but of a *municipium*. No particularly noteworthy event is recorded in its history prior to the earthquake

in 62 A.D. and the fatal eruption by which it was buried in the year 79. This was caused not by the fall of the ashes and small stones that blanketed Pompeii and the whole southern side of Vesuvius, but by an unconsolidated, fluid alluvial mass of lavic material that was swept down from the crater and slopes of Vesuvius to the coast by the torrential rains that accompanied and followed the eruption itself. Initially liquid and muddy, this mass, on penetrating every corner, every house, every room of the city, dried and hardened into a tufa-like stone, enclosing it below a huge petrified stratum some twelve or more metres thick. Yet this, while making the excavation of the site extremely difficult, also had the advantage of creating more favourable conditions of conservation: where the flood did not destroy or sweep them away, the upper floors of the houses in fact remained embedded in the tufa stratum and, by much the same phenomenon that preserves wood in peat-bogs, the wooden parts of the houses have been preserved intact - their beams, their stairways, their doors, their furniture, and even the delicate fibre of textiles and papyrus.

Thus the discovery of Herculaneum occurred as a consequence of the very circumstances which had led to its being

buried, and the early history of the excavations was nothing but an exploration by means of shafts and tunnels almost as if it were a mine from which to extract paintings and sculptures, leaving the buildings submerged for ever. The excavations were begun in a clandestine manner by the Austrian Prince Elboeuf (1709-1716). They were begun in an official form in 1738, with proper directors and skilled workers. By a series of subterranean shafts and galleries, the buildings of the Forum and a good part of the city were explored, culminating in the exploration (1750-65) of the famous Villa of the Papyri, from which bronze and marble sculpture and a library of papyri were recovered. Interrupted in 1765, the excavations were resumed in 1828, abandoning the tunnelling technique and adopting the system of uncovering, as had long been the case at Pompeii, and continued with meagre results until 1875. Finally in 1927 a modern and more rational programme of excavations was begun. Backed up by the necessary works of conservation and restoration for the reintegration of the monuments, it has been conducted methodically right up to the present day. And today, now that a large part of the city has been disinterred, we can finally speak of the rebirth of Herculaneum.

Herculaneum

- Cardo III
- Argus' House
- The House of the Tuscan Colonnade
- Decumanus Maximus
- The Bicentenary House
- Cardo IV
- The House of the Beautiful Courtyard

8 - The House of Neptune and Amphitrite
9 - The House of the Carbonized Furniture
10 - The Baths
11 - The Samnite House
12 - The House of the Wooden Partition
13 - The House of the Mosaic Atrium

14 - The Trellised House
15 - The House of the Great Portal
16 - The Great Gymnasium
17 - Cardo V
18 - The House of the Deers
19 - Suburban Baths
20 - The House of Telephus' Relief
21 - The Lower Decumanus
22 - Apsed Hall

23 - Aristides House
24 - Hotel's House
25 - House of the two Atriums
26 - House of the Alcove
27 - House of the Gem
28 - Augustans' Shrine
29 - The Genius' House
30 - Sacred Area
31 - Upper Hall

HOUSE OF ARGUS

The House of Argus, together with the House of Aristides and the House of the Genius, forms part of the houses of the western quarter, which were the first to be excavated in the modern sense, and which marked, by the abandonment of tunnelling, the beginning of Herculaneum's revival. Uncovered during the excavations of the first period between 1828 and 1865, this house derives its name from a fresco of Io guarded by Argus which decorated the room of the peristyle, but of which no trace remains. The house, which must have been one of the finest and grandest patrician residences in the city, presents a large peristyle or colonnaded court which opens out onto the garden on three sides; the triclinium (dining-room) and other minor rooms face onto it. Of particular interest is the upper part of the house with living quarters and pantries containing the carbonized remains of foodstuffs. This storey overlooking the street and supported on projecting beams, provides valuable evidence of ancient building techniques.

HOUSE OF THE MOSAIC ATRIUM

The House of the Mosaic Atrium is one of the finest houses in what might be called the panoramic district of the city, i.e. laid out along the southern edge of the promontory and commanding a view of the coast and the gulf beyond. The house derives its name from the decoration of the floor of its atrium, consisting of a mosaic with a simple geometric design of black and white squares. A striking feature of the house from an architectural point of view is the fact that the living quarters do not face onto the atrium and the tablinum, but are arranged at right angles to them: an arrangement determined both by the available space and by the panoramic views that could be enjoyed from the town's southern escarpment. A portico with windows, in which many carbonized remains of wooden looms were preserved, leads into the area of the garden, onto which face four small bedrooms and an exedra adorned with decorations. The patrician apartment of the owner of the house extends along the southern wing; it comprises a magnificent triclinium, a series of smaller rooms with elegant decorations, a covered loggia and an open terrace looking towards the sea.

HOUSE OF OPUS CRATICIUM

(Casa a Graticcio)

This house has a façade preceded by portico and a loggia. An example unique in ancient domestic architecture as a whole of a house destined for several families and containing several apartments, it comprises in fact two small independent quarters: one on the groundfloor, to which access was given

House of the Mosaic Atrium.

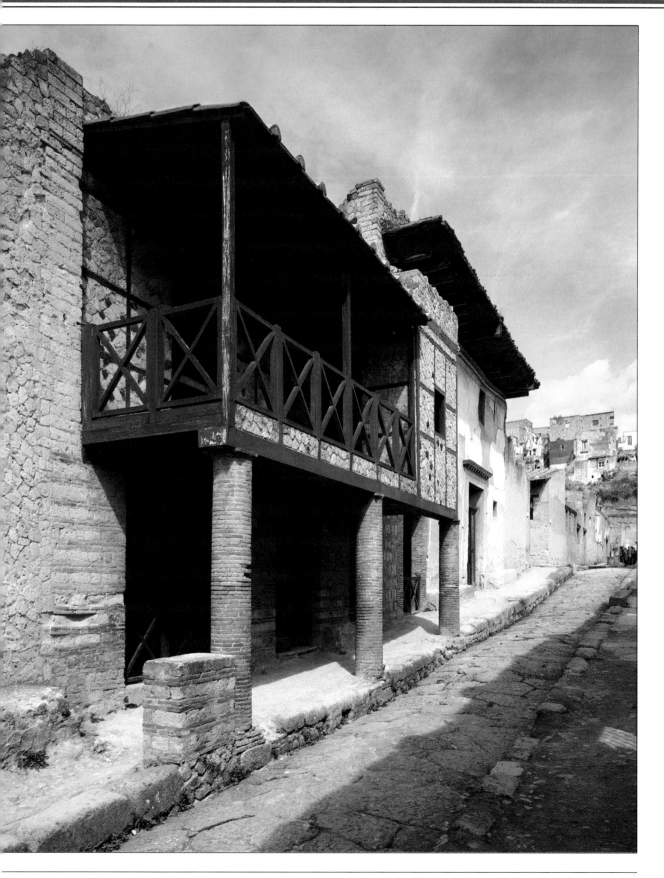

House of Opus Craticium.

by a long passage connected with a craftsman's shop, and the other on the upper floor with small bedrooms, kitchen and gallery overlooking the street. Inside we do not find the usual atrium. In its place is a small courtyard, closed by a high parapet; it served both to provide light to the rooms and to collect the rainwater dripping from the eaves. The replacement of the atrium by the courtyard represents the necessary condition for the transition from the typical domus, inhabited by one family alone, to a house comprising several dwellings. The house derives its name from the *opus Craticium* by which its walls were built. This is a building technique by which the walls are made of a framework of wood or trellis of reeds, filled in with rubble and a good deal of lime. Walls of this type are the "parietes craticii" which Vitruvius lists among the various kinds of structure.

Upper Cardo IV

The street known as Upper Cardo IV is flanked by many large shops, which testify vividly to ancient town life in Herculaneum. One of the most characteristic and interesting is one in which not only the usual counter has been preserved, but also wooden shelves, amphorae and other vessels containing carbonized foodstuffs. Bordered by high pavements, Cardo IV intersects with the Decumanus Maximus.

House of the Wooden Partition

This house too dates to the Samnite period, and has retained its original appearance, even though it was subjected to various alterations around the mid-1st century A.D. In fact a part of it with two street frontages, one on the Lower Decumanus and the other on the Cardo, was transformed into shops and other apartments. The fact that à second floor was added with a separate entrance is evidence, moreover, of the gradual transition from the patrician domus designed for only one family to a house shared by several families. This transition is connected both with changing social conditions and different urbanistic needs. A striking feature of the house is that it retains its external

Upper Cardo IV.

House of the Wooden Partition.

Central Baths.

açade completely preserved right up to its second storey, including its entrance-door, windows and light-holes; it is in fact one of the most complete examples of architectural façade in the houses of both Herculaneum and Pompeii. Yet the most unusual feature of the house, and the one from which it derives its name, is the large partition of carbonized wood, with three doors, that enclosed the wide opening of the tablinum.

THE CENTRAL BATHS

The Central Baths, situated between the Lower Decumanus and the Decumanus Maximus, in the southern part of Insula 6, represented the main bath-house building in Herculaneum. The town was also provided with another bath-house complex, the so-called Suburban Baths, because situated outside the town proper; these are described below. Built in the early Augustan period, around the year 10 A.D., but decorated at a later period, under Claudius or Nero, the Central Baths stood almost in the centre of the town, just a short distance away from the public buildings and the street of the Forum. Larger than the Baths of Pompeii, these Baths of Herculaneum are characterized by much the same division and distribution of the rooms. But as an architectur-

al ensemble they also have greater organic unity as a result of the fact that, unlike those of Pompeii, they did not undergo any alterations from the time of their original construction to that of their burial. As usual in such buildings, the Baths are divided into two sections: one for men and the other for women. The latter is smaller, less decorated and less complete. The male baths are entered from Cardo III: a long narrow corridor leads to the portico of the Palaestra (gymnasium), whence direct access is given to the apodyterium, the changing-room which is surrounded by seats and brackets for hanging clothes. A large marble labrum (basin) is placed

Central Baths.

against the end wall, and close to it was a small rectangular basin, of which only a small parapet remains. The labrum and basin were perhaps used for partial ablutions before entering the inner rooms of the baths. The apodyterium led, to the left, into the frigidarium and, to the right, the tepidarium. The frigidarium is a small circular chamber; it contains a circular basin for cold baths, and is painted with motifs taken from marine fauna: morays, big mullets, garfish and a scene of combat between an octopus and a moray. The large room of the tepidarium, whose mosaic floor is decorated with a Triton surrounded by four dolphins, led in turn into the cali-

darium, with the hot-water basin for immersion on one side and the podium for the cold-water labrum on the other. A small gymnasium, sunny and well-sheltered, completes the installations of the building. The female section of the Baths had a different entrance, located on Cardo IV, but otherwise repeats the same distribution of rooms. The part reserved for women is in fact the better preserved, and retains a delicate and intimate atmosphere. The decoration of the rooms repeats, albeit in a minor mode, the forms and motifs of that of the men's baths. Thus the mosaic floor in the changing-room presents another version of the motif of the

Triton, surrounded by a cupid, four dolphins, an octopus and a cuttle-fish. Simpler in style are the decorations of the tepidarium and the calidarium. Both the men's and women's sections of the Baths were served by the same heating system. The water contained in big boilers was heated to evaporation point, and the hot air was then circulated through the rooms either in the interspace between two superimposed floors or in cavities or air ducts specially built into the walls or vaults.

SAMNITE HOUSE

Situated right opposite the entrance to the Central Baths, the Samnite House dates to the last decades of the 2nd century B.C.. It thus belongs to the end of the pre-Roman period, prior to the outbreak of the Social War (120-100 B.C.) and the constitution of the town as a Roman *municipium*. In fact this house provides the clearest and best-preserved example of a domestic building of Samnite type. The handsome portal built of tufa blocks, with Corinthian capitals and lentil-ornamented cornice, leads into the vestibule adorned by decoration in the 1st style, with stucco rustication painted in imitation of marble. Yet what is of particular interest in the house is its atrium: alongside characteristic features of Italic structure, such as the floor in *opus signinum*, the large opening of the tablinum and the presence of one wing, we find in it a harmonious development of one of the finest motifs of Hellenistic architecture, namely, the portico with ionic columns and openwork screens. Apart from the rooms on the ground-floor, all of them elegantly decorated, the house also has an upper floor comprising two small apartments.

House of the Carbonized Furniture

Situated between the House of Neptune and Amphitrite and the House of the Loom (a combined house and workshop of merchants and producers of cloth), again on Cardo IV, is the so-called House of the Carbonized Furniture. It derives its name from the wooden furniture that is still preserved in its bedroom. Small but elegant, the house, even after having been extensively remodelled following the damage sustained during the earthquake of 62 A.D., exhibits the essential features of pre-Roman structure and the traditional lines of the Domus.

The large entrance doorway, the architectural layout of the atrium which retains the column-supported loggia of the traditional Samnite house, and the arrangement of the rooms round the atrium and inner courtyard, all reveal the character of a house that remained faithful to the plan and structure of the ancient patriarchal dwelling. To the right of the entrance is the triclinium, with rich mural decorations in the 4th style and a polychrome marble floor; these were entirely renewed after 62 A.D. To the left is the bedroom preceded by an ante-chamber. At the far end of the atrium is an elegant tablinum, richly decorated with wall paintings representing female figures. Yet the most interesting part of the house is the bedroom that faces onto the little courtyard with three windows.

It contains a large divan-bed, originally upholstered in furs, and a small table of carbonized wood, its feet carved with the heads of greyhounds.

The room is cool and quiet, and perhaps the owners of the house used to eat their meals here during the hottest days of summer.

The small courtyard of the house is intimate and of great charm; it is enlivened by flower-beds and shrubbery that continue to germinate. At its far end is the Lararium, or shrine of the household gods, which was built during Herculaneum's final years and adorned with fine decorations.

House of the Carbonized Furniture.

HOUSE OF NEPTUNE AND AMPHITRITE

No less beautiful than the luxurious patrician residences, and more intimate, if simpler, in style, are the houses of the middle classes. Once they had become rich by the practice of trade, these people did not abandon the shop associated with their own house, as in the House of Neptune and Amphitrite.

The beauty of its interior, the magnificence of its atrium, the luxuriousness of some of its rooms, reveal the truly refined taste of its owner, who seems, in spirit and custom, to have anticipated the affluent merchants of the Italian Renaissance; they too liked to have a beautiful house, adorned with magnificent works of art, next to their shops. The most interesting part of this house is undoubtedly its small inner courtyard, whose walls are ornamented with a very fine mosaic decoration, vivid in its chromatic effect; this is a rare example of mosaic mural decoration, which was widespread in antiquity, but now completely lost. At the centre is a triclinium built of brickwork with marble revetment.

To the rear is a nymphaeum, formed by a central niche with two small rectangular niches at its sides. Elegant vine-shoot motifs rising from below decorate the jambs of the niches, while festoons of foliage and fruit, and scenes of hunting with deer and hounds, adorn the frieze. The cornice above reproduces the masks of Oceanus and Chimaeras, surrounded by flowers. The wall facing the entrance to the house is in turn decorated with a large mosaic picture representing Neptune and Amphitrite side by side in a shell-shaped pavilion. The statuesque pose of the figures, their academic composure, is enlivened by the extraordinary polychromy of the mosaic itself, so vivid and bright in colour.

Beyond the courtyard, at the far end of the atrium, are the tablinum and a reception- or dining-room.

The house also had an upper floor, whose rooms are visible from the street, since the outer wall collapsed as a result either of the earthquake that accompanied the eruption, or the impact of the river of mud.

*House of **Neptune** and **Amphitrite**.*

26

Workshop adjoining the house of Neptune and Amphitrite.

HOUSE OF THE BEAUTIFUL COURTYARD

Though small, this house is one of the most interesting examples of private Herculanean building. The courtyard, which takes the place of the usual atrium, is architecturally the most unusual and striking part of the house: full of light and colour, it is adorned with a fine mosaic pavement decorated with swastikas in panels. A staircase, provided with pluteus and gallery, leads to the upper floor. Yet it was in the large ground-floor room that the material of greatest interest was found during the excavations: coins, cult statuettes, bronze vessels, glassware, terracottas and small marble sculptures.

HOUSE OF THE TUSCAN COLONNADE

Dating to the Samnite period, this house was built out of large tufa blocks according to the technique of the period. It was readapted during the early imperial period, and restored after the earthquake of 62 A.D., though without losing its original characteristics, even though two rooms were transformed into shops. While the atrium, tablinum and its adjacent rooms are of traditional type, beyond them the house opens up into a large and magnificent peristyle surrounded by colonnades of the Tuscan order, from which the house derives its name. Round the peristyle were arranged the large show rooms, the triclinium and the living quarters, as was the case in all the patrician residences. That this house undoubtedly belonged to a rich family of Herculaneum is shown by the fact that it stood on the main street of the city, and by the discovery in the house of gold coins, the only ones so far found at Herculaneum. Of considerable interest are the wall paintings, belonging to the 3rd and 4th styles.

DECUMANUS MAXIMUS

The main thoroughfare of the town was the Decumanus Maximus, which

27

House of the Tuscan Colonnade.

ran from west to east and crossed the Forum. Some 12 to 14 metres broad and flanked by wide pavements, it was in fact a pedestrianized street, as is shown by the travertine pillars that barred entrance to wheeled vehicles at both its ends, and also by the one or two steps at the intersections with the *cardines* ascending from the southern quarters of the city to the Forum, which effectively limited access to pedestrians alone; by one of these intersections an edict painted on a pillar threatened anyone who dirtied the place with fines and corporal punishment.

The Decumanus constituted the centre of the economic and political life of Herculaneum. The first stretch of the street, which begins from the crossroads of the Fountain of Her-

cules, was flanked by an uninterrupted series of shops and workshops identified by painted signs, and containing earthenware and various utensils. Also facing onto the street were some of the most beautiful residences of Herculaneum such as the House of the Bicentenary and the House of the Black Salon. On its northern side stood a columned portico with brick pillars, illuminated by little windows placed above the intercolumniations. Two floors of houses rose over the portico, while behind it were the entrances to the houses and shops.

Since the houses of the modern town of Ercolano are built over this quarter of the ancient city, it has not been possible to pursue the excavations any further. But the patient and

painstaking process of excavations o those parts of it that are accessibl has permitted the recovery of the va ious wooden components of th buildings: the horizontal beams tha supported the roof of the portico, th jambs and panels of the doors an the shutters of the small windows.

A magnificent four-way arch, face with marble and stucco revetment and with the main barrel-vau flanked by pedestals that supporte toga-clad or equestrian statue marked the passage from the marke Forum to the civil Forum, whic opened up between two porticoe and was paved with a sumptuou marble floor.

To the east of the Forum stood th most noble public building of Herc laneum, the Basilica, while to i outh were situated a large basilical-lan hall and an unusual building that erved as the seat of the College of ugustali. Adjacent to the Forum area as also the Theatre, which was situ-ted at the edge of the north-west art of the town, in the vicinity of a mple.

HOUSE OF THE BICENTENARY

ituated, as we have already men-oned, on the main street of Hercula-eum, the House of the Bicentenary as one of the largest and most sump-ious of the Forum area and of the city s a whole. Belonging to one of the rich-st and most important families of erculaneum, its name derives from e fact that its excavation was complet-d in 1938, i.e. two centuries after the art of the first excavations of Hercula-

neum. What is very striking is the regu-larity of its architectural layout and the grandeur of its private quarters on the ground floor, in spite of the transforma-tions and adaptations to which the house was subjected during its last years of life before the town was buried. From the vestibule, through the fauces, we pass into the large and austere atri-um, which is square in shape with a cen-tral compluvium into which the rainwa-ter drained from the roof. It has a mo-saic floor with a black background, while its walls are painted with a simple decoration in the 4th style, consisting of a black dado and porphyry red panels bearing flying and rampant animals at the centre. At the far end of the atrium two wings open out; the one to the right, instead of being open as usual, is closed by a big wooden gate surmount-

ed by a rich cornice, it too made of wood. What purpose the gate served is unclear: perhaps it was placed here to protect the *imagines maiorum*, since it was the custom in patrician houses to place these in the wings of the atrium, or to guard an archive or a strongbox, but nothing was found to help us under-stand what the original purpose of the wing was. We then pass into the tablinum, the most luxurious and most artistically decorated room in the house, and also the best preserved. Its marble floor has a large rectangular in-laid panel, framed and spread out like a precious polychrome carpet. The deco-ration of the walls constitutes the rich-est complex of painting in the 4th style so far found in the city, of considerable interest for its elegance of design and the abundance of its decorative ele-

ecumanus Maximus.

House of the Bicentenary.

ments. Figural panels are depicted with the myth of Daedalus and Pasiphae on one wall, and that of Venus and Mars on the other. Medallions with busts of satyrs, sileni and bacchantes are placed on the sides of the panels, while a frieze of cupids runs along the cornice on top. The tablinum gives access in turn to the portico with a garden and a series of rustic rooms. In marked contrast to the sumptuousness and luxuriousness of the ground floor are the humble living quarters on the upper floor, which were reached by a small stairway. Originally reserved for a family of servants, at a later stage these rooms were probably rented out to a family of merchants or craftsmen, who ran a small shop in the vicinity of the house. And it is just in a little room of

this upper floor that the sign of the Cross has been found, deeply scored into a stucco panel. Below it is a low wooden cupboard with a footrest, like a domestic oratory. The discovery is of the greatest importance, because it shows that the spread of Christianity to Herculaneum pre-dates 79 A.D. and can probably be traced back to the preaching of the apostle Paul, who landed at Pozzuoli in 61 A.D.

HOUSE OF THE LARGE PORTAL

The large portal from which the house derives its name is undoubtedly the finest entrance-door revealed during the excavations of Herculaneum. It is flanked by brick semicolumns, originally stuccoed and painted red, and surmounted by travertine capitals

adorned with figures of winged vict ries. The house is datable to betwee 26 and 79 A.D. Its interior, though n very large, testifies nonetheless to th prosperity of its owner, as exemplifie by the elegance of its rooms and the r finement of its decorations. In place the atrium we find a long vestibule o to which the various living quarte open. A small open courtyard is situa ed next to the entrance, while opposi it is the most beautiful room of th house: a combined drawing-room ar triclinium, it is adorned with fine pair ings in the 4th style, representi Dionysian themes. Adjacent to it is small but elegant exedra with paintin representing cupids and birds am gardens in flower. Also facing onto t little courtyard is another very elega

ouse of the Bicentenary.
ouse of the Large Portal.

drawing-room, with fine decorations on its walls and a marble panelled floor.

LARGE PALAESTRA

Large in extent and divided into various rooms, the Large Palaestra or Gymnasium is a huge rectangular area extending for more than 80 metres and occupying an entire insula in the eastern quarter of the town. At the intersection of the Lower Decumanus with Cardo V is situated a large vestibule supported by two columns, similar to the pronaos of a temple, which leads into the Palaestra. Another large vestibule is situated at the northern end of the building, close to the Decumanus Maximus. It provides the entrance to a large rectangular hall which leads in turn, through other rooms, all of them finely decorated, to a covered loggia facing onto the area of the Palaestra. It was in this portico that the most important authorities and leading citizens took their seats to watch the games that took place in the gymnasium, while the cryptoporticus provided a convenient shelter for the young athletes waiting for the various competitive events. Surrounded on three sides by a colonnaded portico, the area proper of the Palaestra has at its centre a large pool, unusually in the shape of a cross and 35 metres long. It served as a swimming-pool, and was fed by a large bronze fountain at its centre, formed by a tree trunk, round which a serpent wreathed, from whose five heads water jetted into the basin below. At the centre of the Palaestra's western portico is situated a large apsidal room which must have been sumptuously decorated; unfortunately only a few traces remain of its *opus sectile* pavement and wall paintings of the 4th style. The end wall of th[e] room opens out into a large nich[e] which was intended to contain th[e] statue of the emperor or prince [to] whom the Palaestra was dedicate[d.] At the centre of the hall is the s[o] called *mensa agonistica*, or ceremoni[al] table in white and grey marble, su[p] ported by trapezophorons in th[e] shape of eagle's claws. In all probabil ity it was in this room that the winne[rs] of the gymnastic contests receive[d] their prizes, and the table served t[o] display the various prizes, e.g. met[al] vases and palms. In the Palaestr[a] too, as in a large part of the norther[n] zone of ancient Herculaneum, the e[x] cavations are still in progress, an[d] many rooms still remain to be unco[v] ered. There is no doubt that th[e] whole complex, homogeneous character and built in the post-Augu[s] tan period, served as a public palae[stra]

Large Palaestra.

ower Cardo V.

a or gymnasium, where Hercula-
eum organized sporting events for
young men. The existence of the
mnasium in the town is confirmed
the mention of gymnastic games in
e honorary decree of Marcus Non-
s Balbo, one of the most influential
izens of Herculaneum, who had al-
filled the post of proconsul. The
vered area of the Palaestra proper
laid out along the inner façade,
ile along the outer façade, looking
to the street, are a series of shops
d houses for rent, with two or more
per floors and containing several
artments.

THE LOWER CARDO V

Cardo V, which led through a gate to the
suburban quarter of Herculaneum, is
flanked by smaller and simpler houses
than the luxurious residences we have
so far described. These houses, more
than one storey in height and divided
into several homes, testify to the existence of a very heterogeneous population in terms of economic and social
conditions.

And an even more immediate and vivid
testimony of the customs and traditions
of the people of Herculaneum is provided by the numerous shops of the

city, in which a variety of commercial
activities took place. There were the
bakeries (*pistrina*) where bread was produced and sold; the *thermopolia* (bars)
and *tabernae* (shops) which sold wine, oil
and various foodstuffs.

There were the workshops and dyers'
shops, and the shops that sold fabrics
and household furnishings. In all these
commercial premises the excavations
have uncovered their typical fittings
and earthenware of every kind, sometimes containing carbonized food. At
the entrance to one tavern - rare testimony indeed -   a painted sign was
found.

HOUSE OF THE DEER

The large House of the Deer, which is situated on the Lower Cardo V, belongs to the series of the panoramic houses of Herculaneum. Indeed it is one of the richest and most elegant of them. The distribution of rooms in it and the utilization of space are subordinated to the needs and habits of its owner and in this respect it represents a further stage in the evolution of the traditional house type. The house consists of a huge rectangle extending longitudinally from north to south. It is subdivided into a northern quarter with a series of rooms leading off from the entrance, and a southern quarter with the terraces open to the sea. Apart from the rooms reserved for servants, the kitchen and the pantry, the northern part comprises a large triclinium and a drawing-room. The southern complex, more extensive and luxurious, consists of the summer triclinium, flanked by two smaller siesta rooms, and ends with a loggia, opening out into a pergola and two other recreational rooms for resting in the afternoon (the so-called "cubicola diurna"). Apart from its symmetrical architectural layout, what is striking in the House of the Deer is the richness and beauty of its decorations. In the northern triclinium the wall paintings belonging to the 4th style, and thus dating to the final decades of life at Herculaneum, consist of fantastic, but highly linear, architectural perspectives, set against a dark background. Along the wings of the inner portico a series of charming little panels represent cupids, still-lifes and mythological subjects. Also very striking in the house is the unusual richness of its floors; these consist of black and white tessellated mosaic along the ambulatories of the four-sided portico, and of marble inlays in the more important rooms. Two large slabs of oriental alabaster are laid out, like precious carpets, in front of the two smaller rooms of the southern quarter. The portal leading from the portico into the inner garden has a pediment decorated with a composition of glass-paste mosaic, with the bearded head of Oceanus at its centre and a frieze of cupids on sea-horses at its sides. The area of the garden was adorned with two groups of deer being attacked by hounds, and it was from these marble sculptures of exceptional beauty that the house took its name. Two other statuettes of very fine workmanship are on display in the house: a "Drunken Hercules", a jocular representation of the mythical hero and legendary founder of the city, and a "Satyr with Wineskin". Small amphorae and other objects found during the excavations are contained in show-cases placed in various rooms in the house. Open to the sea and to the wide crescent of the Gulf, the House of the Deer dates to the Claudio-Neronian period, as is attested by its structure and decorations, even though it underwent restoration after the earthquake in 62 A.D.

House of the Deer - The Satyr with te wineskin.

HOUSE OF THE RELIEF OF TELEPHUS

This is the largest and most luxurious house in the southern quarter, and also the most unusual, due to its markedly oblique plan; this was made necessary to adapt the building to the irregularity and declivity of the ground. The atrium, unconventional in shape and resembling more the forms of Hellenistic architecture, is surrounded by a portico with the rooms of the upper floor above it. It has a high-rimmed rectangular basin, instead of the impluvium, at its centre. The walls and columns are adorned with a decoration against a red background and a group of marble *oscilla* (masks) representing Dionysian and theatrical themes. From this sector the house a corridor descends to th luxurious quarter on the lower floo which is oriented obliquely to the fo mer. Here the peristyle supported b brick columns surrounds a large ga den, which has at its centre a recta gular basin faced with plaster on blue background. Various rooms op onto the peristyle; they presumab comprised a dining-room, a drawin room and a bedroom. Of these th largest, and certainly the finest, is th one adorned with marble decoratic of exceptional beauty: the most sum tuous known to us from a priva house in antiquity. The room still tains the marble revetment of its wa scotting, in which horizontal and ve

ouse of the **Deers**.

House of the **Relief** *of* **Telephus** .

cal panels consist of alternating
oolin, pavanazzetto and African mar-
e slabs, surrounded by border strips
d articulated by small pillars with
orinthian capitals. The use of
loured marbles, the richness of the
coration, the elegance of the archi-
ctural and geometric motifs, all
monstrate the particular affluence
d refined taste of the owner of the
ouse, which must have been
orned with numerous other works of
t, destroyed or dispersed by the fury
the flood. However, one significant
ork of art was discovered in a little
om adjacent to the sumptuous salon
e have just described. It consists of a
eo-Attic relief representing the myth
Telephus, from which the house de-
ves its name. No less distinguished
e the two fine reliefs of four-horsed
ariots, which were evidently trans-
orted here from another building by
e deluge of mud, and which have
en reassembled from numerous
agments. They are displayed in the
rium of the house and symbolize the
ternation of day and night in the per-
nifications of Phosphoros and Hes-
eros riding a quadriga.

SUBURBAN BATHS

Less extensive and of more recent construction than the Central Baths, the Suburban Baths are situated outside the area of the city proper; they abut onto the outer walls of the House of the Gemstone and the House of the Relief of Telephus in the southern part of the town. These baths are the most interesting discovery of the recent excavations. Being situated at a level far lower than that of the town itself, they were not only covered by a thicker and even harder alluvial stratum, but had been flooded by groundwater up to a considerable height, either because the ancient drainage channels to the sea had become blocked, or due to phenomena of bradyseism. This meant that the work of excavation was particularly difficult, even though its end result has been to restore to us one of the best preserved bath-house complexes in the ancient world. The simple façade of the building looks onto a square, in which stands the monument in honour of the proconsul M. Nonius Balbo, by whom the baths were probably built. On entering the baths through the façade, and on descending some steps, we are admitted to the vestibule, which has the shape of a tetrastyle atrium with the columns surmounted by two orders of arches. Light floods down directly from the light-hole above, illuminating the room in a most suggestive way. A marble herm of Apollo is placed against a pillar, from which water descended into the basin below. Adjacent to the vestibule is a kind of recreational room, without bathing facilities but with marble seats arranged all round. It is enriched by an elegant decoration of exceptional quality. The white stuccoed walls are divided into large panels with cornices, surrounded by plant-motif ornamentations and bearing the figure of a warrior at the centre. Contrasting with the white walls is the carmine red of the frieze that runs round the top of the walls, and the vivid colours of the marble wainscot and floor. The usual component rooms of the Baths are systematically arranged and in a perfect state of preservation: the apodyterium (changing room), the frigidarium, the calidarium, equipped with a small pool and a basin for ablutions, the tepidarium connected with the laconicum, the small circular room for steam baths (a kind of sauna), and the praefurnium where the water-heating plant was situated.

Suburban Baths: the frigidarium.

uburban baths: the vestibulum with the herma of Apollo.

Apse of the Basilica: Theseus defeating the minotaur (Archaeological Museum in Naples).

Basilica: Hercules recognizes his son (Archaeological Museum in Naples).

POMPEII: THE FASCINATION OF THE PAST

The panorama of Pompeii is dominated by the proud and solitary cone of Vesuvius, the arbiter and witness of its life and death. Laid out at its feet, the silent remains of the long-buried city are charged with the vivid fascination of history and conjure up, with extraordinary immediacy, a distant past. The destiny of Pompeii has been a unique one. This flourishing Campanian city was completely submerged and destroyed in 79 A.D. by the eruption of the volcano, which covered it completely by a stratum of ash and small stones up to a depth of metres. It is just the nature of this material spewed forth by the volcano, far lighter in consistency than lava, that has enabled the city to be disinterred in its entirety and ensured that not only its architectural features and pictorial decorations, but also its furnishings, household articles, the most varied implements of trade, even foodstuffs and textiles, have been preserved intact. Pompeii has thus yielded a complex of finds of extraordinary importance and richness, as well as of exceptional fascination, because they provide a picture of everyday life in ancient times which is truly unique. A great many ancient cities, monuments and archaeological finds have been brought back to light and diligently recomposed by scholars, like pieces of a jigsaw to reconstruct the material appearance of ancient civilizations. The case of Pompeii is different: from that stratum of ash which, in the space of a few minutes, suffocated and destroyed a city and its population almost two thousand years ago, a whole civilization has today re-emerged intact. It has yielded, as if from embalmment, an entire urban nucleus consisting not only of houses, temples and public buildings, but also countless little things that tell us vividly about the customs, habits, life-styles and day-to-day activities of people from all walks of life: both the important and the ordinary; both the rich and the poor. All of a sudden, the city was cancelled from history by the eruption of Vesuvius; everything was stopped in its tracks in a flash. Now, so many centuries later, Pompeii once more stands before us: disinterred from ash, it has been restored to our sight, thus enabling us to grasp the images of its past, and to rediscover not only the moments of its tragedy and death, but also those of its day-to-day life. It is just this that constitutes the peculiarity of Pompeii: its capacity to furnish us with a comprehensive, exhaustive and above all vivid picture of a civilization of the past. No other documentation is so vivid, so immediate and so clear as that provided by the thousands of finds recovered during the excavations of Pompeii. No other monument, no matter how grand and important, is able to tell the same things; no written testimony is able to be so explicit about the everyday life of a city as does a visit to Pompeii where we can wander through its streets, enter its homes and come into contact with the everyday objects that characterized it. At Pompeii we are able to observe how they washed and wove cloth, how they milled flour and made bread, how they carried out electoral propaganda or encouraged the participation of the population in the entertainments held in the Theatre or Amphitheatre. We are able to discover how they were organized: their bars or gambling dens and also their shops which were generally situated on the ground floor of their houses. We are even able to reconstruct how they spent their leisure activities, whether in the Baths or in the gymnasia, or strolling through the streets and in the Forum to discuss politics, business and justice.

Another type of documentation of great importance provided by the disinterred city is that concerning the life and habits of the various social classes. The types of houses are extremely significant in this regard. It is in fact possible to distinguish the house of the noble family from that of the mercantile and industrial class, and that in turn from the house of the people. The first of these conforms to the classic Roman typology (which we will discuss in more detail below). The second, while substantially repeating the main features of the *domus*, is generally distinguished by two characteristics: that of being particularly luxurious as a way of evincing the importance and standing achieved by the bourgeoisie, and that of removing the house proper to the first floor in order to leave room on the ground floor for the shop. Thirdly, the houses of the people: these are far smaller and more modest, without decorations and often provided with gardens in which the essential produce of the earth was cultivated. Servants and slaves had no house of their own; they were allocated instead some small rooms in the service area which every high-class home was equipped with. There were also hotels and rented accommodation for people in transit, who must have been numerous in Pompeii in view of the city's mercantile and trading activities and thriving business as a port. The town's well-to-do districts and those of the people can be distinguished: the former were traversed by broad, paved streets, flanked by the façades of handsome and affluent villas, in whose interiors splendid gardens and magnificent decorations could be glimpsed. The heavily-built up popular districts, by contrast, were penetrated by narrow, badly-surfaced alleyways, wedged between simple and low-lying little houses flanked by small shops. To understand and appreciate Pompeii we need therefore not just to confine our attention to its most significant monuments and buildings from an artistic viewpoint, but explore it in its entirety: only in this way shall we be able to discover its true face, re-live its past, and allow ourselves to be gripped by all the evocativeness of the countless things that so vividly conjure up its centuries-old history.

POMPEII: HISTORICAL BACKGROUND

Pompeii stands on a lava plateau created as a result of one of the many eruptions of Vesuvius in the distant past. It was probably founded by the Oscan inhabitants of Campania, who chose this raised plateau because it had the advantage of being naturally defended and at the same time not far from the sea. This factor undoubtedly favoured the economic and political development of the city, which subsequently succumbed to the influence of the Greeks who had extended their rule to a large part of southern Italy and in particular to the Gulf of Naples where they had established powerful strongholds and naval bases. For a brief period (525-474 B.C.) the city was subjected to the Etruscans, but after the latter's defeat at Cumae, was restored once again to the rule of the Greeks. The struggle between these two peoples for supremacy in the territory of Campania was resolved by the intrusion of another civilization, that of the Samnites, who succeeded in extending their rule over many cities, including Pompeii, which now underwent the reconstruction and enlargement of its town centre. The archaeological excavations have in fact revealed a number of buildings of Italic-Samnite type, as well as various sculptural and pictorial works referable to the same period. The influence of Greek art is, however, detectable in some temples, in the decoration of some interiors, and in part of the circuit of walls by which the city was surrounded.

Already in the 4th century B.C. Campania began to be penetrated by Roman troops who sought to gain domination over southern Italy. This precipitated three Samnite wars which ended with the victory of Rome and the subjection of these territories to her rule. Pompeii shared the same fate: at first it was declared "socia" - an ally or confederate - of Rome and was thus granted a degree of autonomy. Later, however, in the year 80 B.C., after having been besieged and defeated following its participation in the Social War undertaken by the Italic peoples in defence of their own independence, Pompeii became a Roman colony with the name of "Colonia Veneria Cornelia Pompeii". From then onwards, the city was, to all intents and purposes, a Roman town in its political and administrative life, as in the development of its forms of building, and in the art of painting and sculpture. In the economic field, Pompeii distinguished itself for its industrial and commercial activities, as was testified by the expansion of its mercantile bourgeoisie.

THE DEATH OF POMPEII

In 62 A.D. Pompeii suffered its first catastrophe: a terrible earthquake struck Campania. Pompeii suffered appalling damage; many of its buildings collapsed or were seriously damaged. The city, however, was economically strong and flourishing and this permitted its recovery: its private houses and public buildings were restored; other new ones were erected; the number of shops grew; and the town's villas were further embellished with a new series of pictorial decorations. But only a few years later, on 24 August 79 A.D., in the early hours of the afternoon - the detailed description is supplied by Pliny the Elder, who died during the catastrophe, in a letter to his nephew - Vesuvius suddenly began to erupt. An enormous mass of volcanic ash and small pumice-stones showered down on the city, burying it completely. The inhabitants attempted flee towards the coast, but died just the same - caught in their flight by the enormous mass of incandescent material spewed forth by the volcano. Those, by contrast, who remained holed up in their houses died suffocation. Of these victims a tangible and gruesome record remains the plaster-casts of their burnt-out cadavers: i.e. the casts produced pouring liquid plaster into the empty spaces left by the decomposition their bodies. As we have already had occasion to point out, the fact that Pompeii was submerged by a blanket of ash has enabled it to be disinterred with relative ease. This was far from being the case at nearby Herculaneum and Stabiae, which were also submerged by the eruption, but were destroyed by the lava. This, progressively solidifying in the course

me, has created serious problems for the carrying out of the excavations and had a deleterious effect on the appearance of these towns and their complete reconstruction. Pompeii thus fell victim to a sudden death in 79 A.D., almost two millennia ago. From then onwards its history has been inseparably bound up with its rediscovery.

THE REDISCOVERY OF POMPEII AND THE HISTORY OF THE EXCAVATIONS

The first rediscovery of Pompeii was made quite accidentally: it occurred in the late 16th century on the occasion of the excavation of a water-conduit close to the river Sarno. The architect Fontana, in charge of the work, found some inscriptions, a few remains of walls and some specimens of ancient painting. At the time, however, it was not inferred from these finds that the site in question could be that of this ancient city, the memory of which had been totally lost.

Other excavations on the site were not carried out till after 1748.

This was at the behest of King Charles III of Bourbon, after other remains of buildings had been revealed, again accidentally. The archaeological exploration of the site then proceeded in a more systematic manner, and since the disinterment of this area proved a great deal easier than that of neighbouring Herculaneum, which had begun a few years previously, attention was almost exclusively concentrated on the business of bringing back Pompeii to light. During the first stage, the Theatre and the tombs of the Via dei Sepolcri were uncovered. Then, in the early years of the 19th century, the Forum area was excavated. After 1860, especially under the superintendence of Giuseppe Fiorelli, a period of more organic and scien-

tific study and excavation was inaugurated; this permitted a large part of the city to be disinterred. At the same time, new archaeological techniques permitted the systematic restoration of the monuments and measures aimed at their more effective conservation. It was to Fiorelli that we owe the ingenious solution of obtaining plaster-casts of the victims of the eruption by pouring liquid plaster into the cavities in the ground. In fact, the bodies of human beings and animals, as well as the most varied household furnishings and objects, had left - as they gradually dissolved - an empty space between the strata of solidified ash. It was just this process that has enabled us today to have so many vivid testimonies of the past and so many realistic and dramatic images of that appalling tragedy Following the work of Fiorelli, other archaeologists, including Ruggiero, Maiuri and others, have continued the excavations. The most recent phases of the disinterment of Pompeii have been characterized by a new system of excavation aimed not only at conserving the surviving masonry of the buildings, but also at reconstituting the missing parts and maintaining paintings, sculptures and objects *in situ*, i.e. without removing them from the site on which they were found and transferring them to Museums. This ensures that the appearance and character of the ancient city remain more intact and more significant in all its aspects.

TOWN PLAN OF POMPEII
BUILDING PERIODS AND TYPES

The town plan of Pompeii is closely related to the nature of the terrain on which it is situated. Since, as we have said, it occupies a lava plateau characterized by a marked incline southwards and by some irregularity in ground level, the structure of the town has had to be accommodated to the sloping terrain. In fact, the only flat area is that of the Forum.

In ancient times, the lava plateau on which Pompeii stands represented a natural defence for the population that had settled there, because this rocky spur prevented access especially from the sea. Yet in spite of this, massive defensive walls were built even at the time of the emergence of the original settlement, and these were subsequently extended during several periods. At the present time, the fortifications of Pompeii, which are fairly well-preserved and almost entirely excavated, form a circuit of over 3 km. and reveal almost everywhere the building technique of Samnite type consisting of large squared blocks, reinforced by an agger or ditch. This defensive circuit of walls is pierced, along its perimeter, by a number of gates, all of them providing direct access to the main thoroughfares of the town: namely, the Porta Marina, Porta Ercolano, Porto Vesuvio, Porta Stabiana, Porta di Nola and Porta Nocera. Another gate was probably situated along the northern perimeter between the Porta Vesuvio and the Porta di Nola. Within this circuit of walls Pompeii discloses a town plan which is substantially one of Roman type: the main streets are the *cardo maximus* (the Via Stabiana) and, at right-angles to it, the *decumanus* (the Via di Nola), which are intersected by other secondary streets, forming an orthogonal grid. In contrast to almost all Roman towns, however, Pompeii's Forum - in other words, the central square flanked by its most important public and religious buildings - is situated towards the west, and hence not actually in the centre of the town. The Forum's off-centre position is to be attributed to the natural lie of the land, for it was only here that a fairly extensive flat area was available.

The Amphitheatre and the large Palaestra, on the other hand, are situated in the eastern part of the town, for it was only on this side that a sufficiently extensive area for buildings of this type was to be found. The oldest nucleus of the town is represented by the buildings of the Triangular Forum and the urban agglomeration immediately to the east of the great Forum. More meticulous and detailed examination of the fabric of Pompeii has permitted various building periods to be identified in the town's architecture, on the basis of a scrutiny of the materials and techniques used. These periods can be summarized as follows:

1) First Period: the houses dating to the first, pre-Samnite period are characterized by their severity and simplicity of style, as well as by the use of sandstone and tufa (soft volcanic rock), materials which could be quarried in proximity to the town.

2) Samnite Period: buildings of this period are still constructed with tufa, sandstone and other volcanic material. But the building technique is more developed, and structures built out of irregular and squared masonry (*opus incertum* and *opus quadraturn*) are found. Influences of Greek type also make themselves felt during this period.

3) Roman Period: characterized by an increasingly skilful use of the same materials encountered in the previous periods with the addition of brick which often assumes a decorative function. As regards the streets, these were almost all paved with large polygonal blocks of stone, closely fitted together. A narrow pavement flanked the houses to permit access to them and the free tran-

sit of pedestrians. Large blocks stone may often be seen jutting u from the street paving; these serve as stepping-stones for pedestrians enable them to walk without gettin their feet wet when the streets wer awash with rain water or drainage has to be noted that the drainage sy tem was in fact not very developed The same function was served by th pavement curbs. The deep ruts of servable along the paving of th streets were left by the passage waggons. Various public fountain were situated at crossroads or abu ting onto one or two houses.

Numerous shops are to be foun flanking the main streets, especial along the Via dell'Abbondanza, a ma jor thoroughfare which attained th height of its importance in concu rence with the marked developmen of the commercial and industri class. Pompeii was in fact thronge with workshops of various type: thos for the washing and dyeing of clot are numerous, as are bakers an millers for the milling of wheat. N less numerous are *tabernae* (sma inns) and *thermopolia* (bars in quite th modern sense), serving for the re freshment of passers-by.

There are shops, too, for the selling fruit and vegetables, shoeshop blacksmiths and even pastry-shops. The urban fabric and the social fabr of Pompeii are everywhere close connected: a knowledge of them co tributes to enlarging and deepenir our picture of this city and its civiliza tion.

POMPEIAN BUILDING

A question that deserves separat discussion is that of Pompeian build ing - not so much public buildin whose distinguishing features are no very different from those disclose by temples, baths, theatres an basilicas in other ancient cities, a private building, which is so wide represented here. This in fact pro vides an incomparably rich and e haustive picture of the architectur development of house-types throug the various periods, ranging from th Italic-Samnite to the Roman perio from the humble abode of the peopl to the sumptuous patrician villa. It may indeed be claimed that no oth er archaeological zone combines suc rich variety of houses, architectural styles and the utilization of space, even the sheer extent and profusion of the finds made at Pompeii. Such is the enormous amount of evidence on house styles at our disposal that it has also been possible to reconstruct the organization of domestic life in the various social strata. It may be worthwhile at this point to give an example of how a typical Roman house was planned and built, so that the visitor, in the course of a tour of the excavations, may have at his disposal a sufficiently clear and indicative blueprint of what such a house was like. The house had a rectangular plan of variable width, sometimes extending even to a whole insula (or block), or sometimes isolated as in the case of some of the more luxurious villas. Externally, it presented no aperture other than the entrance. The house was entered through the vestibulum or entrance-way (1), which normally jutted out into the street. This led into the Fauces (2) or entrance passage, through which one passed into the Atrium or forecourt (3). This was a rectangular or square space with, at its centre, the Impluvium (4) or cistern into which the rainwater drained from the roof. Round the Atrium, which constituted the central nucleus of the house, a series of rooms known as Cubicula (5) were arranged; these generally formed the living quarters of members of the

family. In some houses, the Atrium was followed by an open apartment known as the Tablinum (6) which assumed a varying function according to period, sometimes serving as a bedroom or a living room. Beyond this extended the Alae or wings (7) and the Peristylium (8); the latter was represented in the first period simply by a garden, but was subsequently developed into a court surrounded by a colonnade and embellished with statues, fountains and plants. Other Cubicula, Oeci or drawing rooms (9) and the Triclinium, which became the new dining room, were arranged round it. With the evolution of the structure and plan of the house, many rooms were enlarged and assumed a different function: for example, the bedrooms and living rooms were doubled in number, and distinguished between summer and winter quarters according to their siting and arrangement. Sometimes, too, the atrium and the peristyle were doubled. Very often private bathhouses were added with separate rooms for the frigidarium, tepidarium and calidarium. Naturally, each house was equipped, in its less important and less easily accessible part, by a series of small rooms for services such as the kitchens, storerooms, cellars and living quarters for the servants. Other houses consist, by contrast, of two storeys: they are those which utilized the ground floor for the shop or workshop and installed the bed-rooms on

the upper floor. Such houses are equipped inside with intermediate floors and internal staircases or even with external galleries. Some suburban villas are furnished with large gardens and windows overlooking the valley below. These villas represent a further evolution of the Pompeian house, which is now opened up on the outside in order to exploit the beauty of the surrounding panorama. This is the case with the famous Villa of the Mysteries and the Villa of Diomedes. As may be observed in the course of a visit to the excavations, the Pompeian house offers a very wide variety of architectural solutions and hence extensive evidence about vernacular building styles in antiquity and the social aspects of domestic life with which they are so closely linked. In touring Pompeii, we have ample opportunity for observing how each house, though obeying in some measure the essential features of the typical house of the period, is organized according to the particular taste of the family that built it and also according to the trends of the moment.

This is true for the architecture and the building techniques. But it is equally true of everything to do with the house's decoration. The decoration, which forms an integral part of the Pompeian house, is indeed of considerable importance for an understanding of ancient civilization as a whole.

PLAN OF THE TYPICAL ROMAN HOUSE

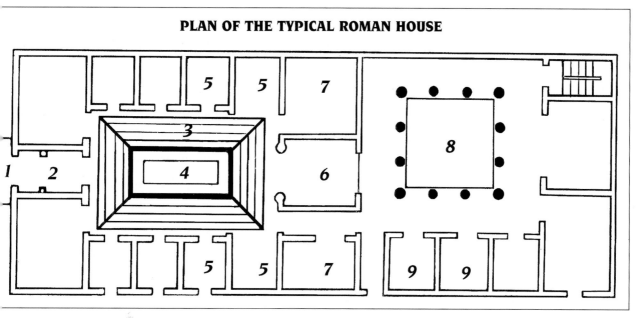

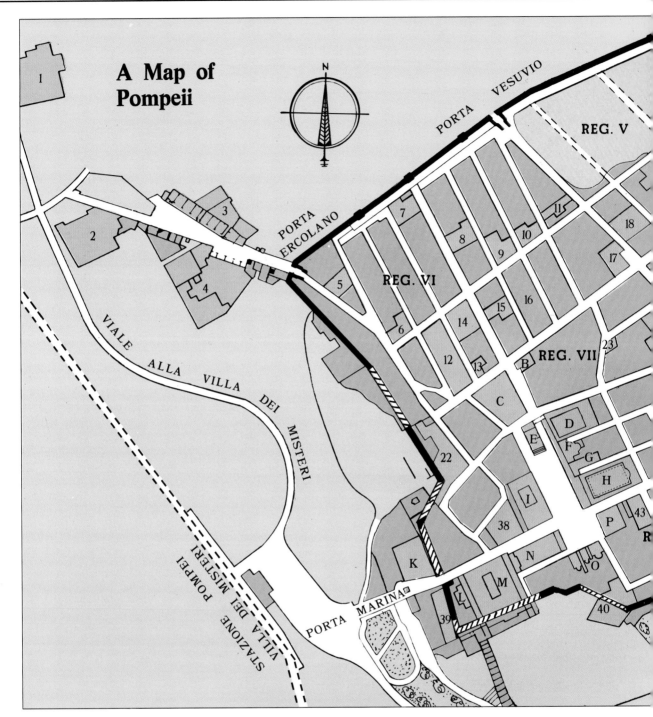

A Map of Pompeii

N

PORTA VESUVIO

REG. V

PORTA ERCOLANO

REG. VI

REG. VII

VIALE ALLA VILLA DEI MISTERI

STAZIONE POMPEI

VILLA DEI MISTERI

PORTA MARINA

PRIVATE EDIFICES

1 - Villa of the Mysteries
2 - Villa of Diomeds
3 - Villa of the Mosaic Columns
4 - Villa of Cicero
5 - House of the Surgeon
6 - House of Sallust
7 - House of Apollo
8 - House of Meleager
9 - House of the Labyrinth
10 - House of the Vettii
11 - House of the Gilded Cupids
12 - House of Pansa
13 - House of the Tragic Poet
14 - House of the Large Fountain and House of

the Small Fountain
15 - House of the Anchor
16 - House of the Faun
17 - House of Orpheus and House of the
Etruscan Column
18 - House of Caecilius Jucundus
19 - House of the Silver Wedding
20 - House of Marcus Lucretius
21 - House of the Gladiators
22 - House of Fabius Rufus
23 - Mill and Oven
24 - House of Gavius Rufus
25 - House of the Bear
26 - Brothel (Lupanare)
27 - Hotel of Sittius
28 - House of Siricus

29 - House of Marcus Lucretius
30 - House of the Centenary
31 - House of Obellius Firmus
32 - House of Epidius Rufus
33 - House of the "peristilio ad Archi"
34 - House of Julius Polybius
35 - House of Trebius Valens
36 - House of Pinarius Cerialis
37 - House of the Moralist
38 - House of Trittolemo
39 - Imperial Villa
40 - Sarno-Baths
41 - Curia Isiaca
42 - House of the emperor "Giuseppe II"
43 - Villa of the Wild Boar
44 - House of Cornelius Rufus

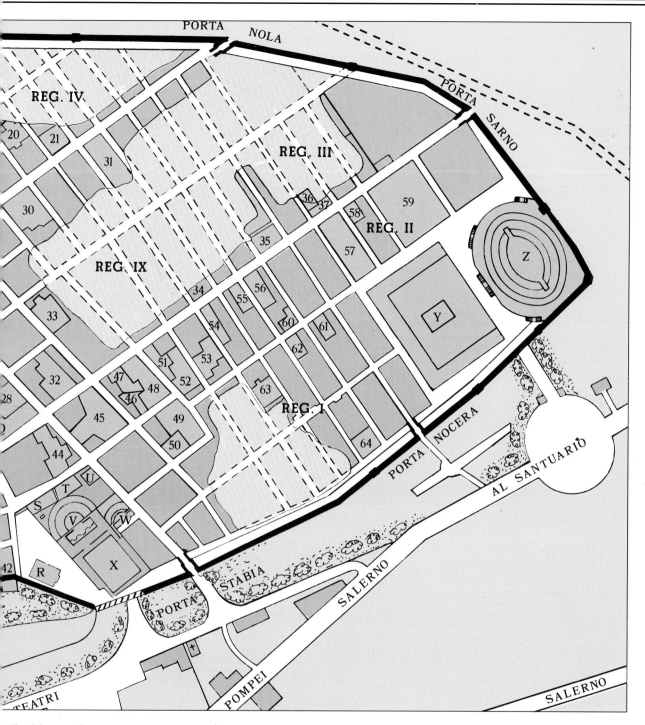

Villa of the Lyre-Player
House of the Ceii
Fullonica Stephani
House of the Cryptoporticus
House of Menander
House of the Lovers
House of Paquius Proculus
House of the Ephebe
House of the four styles
House of the Impluvium
House of Venus "in Bichini"
Oven and Mills of Sotericus
House of Loreius Tiburtinus
House of Venus
Villa and Baths of Julia Felix
Workshop of Garum

61 - House of the Lararium of Sarnus
62 - House of the "Nave Europa"
63 - House of the Arches
64 - Garden of the Fugitives

PUBLIC EDIFICES

A - Central Baths
B - Temple of Fortune
C - Forum Baths
D - Macellum
E - Temple of Jupiter
F - Temple of the Lares
G - Temple of Vespasian
H - Edifice of Eumachia
I - Temple of Apollo
K - Suburban Baths

L - Museum (Antiquarium)
M - Temple of Pompeian Venus
N - Basilica
O - Curie
P - Comitium
Q - Stabian Baths
R - Doric Temple
S - Samnite Palaestra
T - Temple of Isis
U - Temple of Jupiter Meilichius
V - Large Theatre
W - Little Theatre
X - Gladiators' Barracks
Y - Great Palaestra
Z - Amphitheatre

ART AT POMPEII: PAINTING, MOSAIC AND SCULPTURE

An essential element of the Pompeian house is above all its pictorial decoration. In view of the richness, variety and extent of the surviving evidence of such decoration, it undoubtedly represents one of the most significant testimonies of the history of ancient art and the evolution of styles through the various periods. Campanian painting is in fact almost the only surviving example of mural painting in the Roman world, and thus offers one of the few secure points of reference for our knowledge of this genre of art during this period. Scholars have identified four different styles of Pompeian pictorial decoration corresponding to four successive periods: Painting of the 1st Style: from the 2nd to the mid-1st century B.C. It is called "incrustation style", and is characterized by polychrome decorations in stucco, which divide the wall surface into panels and try to resemble facings of different coloured marbles. The colours black, red and yellow generally predominate. Examples of this style may be found in the Villa of the Mysteries, that of the Labyrinth, and that of the Silver Wedding. Painting of the 2nd Style: from the mid-1st century B.C. to the early years of the 1st century A.D. It is known as the "architectural style" (or "painting in architectural perspective"), the wall surfaces being depicted with illusionistic architectural perspectives. Various compositions, ranging from landscapes to large figural scenes with a mythological or religious content, are inserted in the empty spaces. The marvellous mural decorations of the Villa of the Mysteries in Pompeii exemplify this style. Painting of the 3rd Style: from the early years of the 1st century A.D. to 62 A.D. It is called the "real wall" or "pseudo-Egyptian style". The architectural features are still present, but now become more slender and graceful to the point of assuming a largely decorative value. The wall surfaces are at the same time enriched with friezes of the most delicate ornament, painted with rapid, luminous brush-strokes. The famous frieze of the "Cupids" from the House of the Vettii is a significant example of this. Painting of the 4th Style: between 62 A.D. and 79 A.D. It goes under the name of "architectural illusionism". Once again the walls are painted with imaginary architectural scenes which create illusions of highly elaborate and recherché landscape and perspective vistas, so much so as to make us think of a baroque taste *ante litteram*. This style of decoration is also exemplified in some rooms of the House of the Vettii. Another major component of Pompeian art, and one that merits separate treatment, is represented by the mosaic so widely used both in the decoration of floors and in that of fountains, impulvia and even walls. For this genre too, we can identify various periods and various styles which testify to the progressive development of the technique and the use of ever more precious materials. One of the largest and most splendid mosaics at Pompeii is the "Battle of Alexander" from the House of the Faun (now displayed in the National Archaeological Museum in Naples). The collection of sculptures found in the course of the excavations is also of the greatest value and variety. In the main, they consist of sculptures in bronze and marble, but terracotta statues have also been found. The influence of Hellenistic art is especially apparent in this field of Pompeian art; indeed, the statuary excavated includes a number of wonderful copies of Greek originals. Of the more important statues we may mention: the "Apollo" and "Diana" from the Temple of Apollo; the "Apollo playing the Lyre" from the House of the Lyre-Player; the bronze "Ephebe" from the House of the Ephebe; the "Dancing Faun" from the House of the Faun; and the "Drunken Silenus". Another sculpture of great interest is the animal group of the "Wild Boar attacked by Hounds" found in the House of the Lyre-Player together with other valuable statues. To help visitors orientate themselves better during their tour of the excavations, we should point out that the town has been divided into regions (9), each of which has been further subdivided into insulae (blocks). Each building in each individual insula has then been identified by a consecutive number. Where appropriate, these are cited in brackets below to help you identify the various buildings.

THE PORTA MARINA

The ancient Porta Neptunia, la[...] commonly called Marina because[...] faces the sea, though it provides [...] most direct access to the Forum ar[...] the town centre and its most imp[...]tant nucleus, was not in fact the m[...] gateway leading into Pompeii. It [...] unsuitable for this purpose, in view[...] the morphology of the terrain whic[...] here fairly steep and thus not sui[...] to the passage of waggons.

The gate is characterized by two b[...]

Porta Marina.
Below: *panoramic view of the For[...] area.*

-vaulted arches; of the two arches,
 e one on the left, which has a steep-
 passageway, was reserved for
ules. A statue of the goddess Min-
va was formerly placed in the niche
 the right. The Porta Marina is one
 the seven gates that have been re-
aled during the excavations. The
hers are: the Porta Ercolano, Por-
Vesuvio, Porta di Nola, Porta di
rno, Porta Nocera and Porta Stabia.
 eighth gate which is no longer vis-
le probably existed between the
rta Nola and Vesuvio.

E Temple of Venus

 which almost nothing still re-
ained at the time of the eruption of
suvius. Venus was the goddess
opted as the protectress of the
wn. Only a few scanty remains and
 e area on which the temple stood
n be seen at the present time. We
 e now in the area of the Forum.

The Forum

The ancient political, economic and
religious centre of Pompeii, the Forum consists of a large rectangular
space (measuring 142x38 metres),
surrounded by a number of important
public buildings. It was here, in this
area, that the civic life of Pompeii was
principally concentrated and was giv-
en its greatest expression. Here in
fact stood the city's major temples,
including the great Temple of Jupiter,
the greatest of its cult buildings.
Here, too, stood the Basilica, Pompeii's most significant public building, the seat of the law-courts and a
trading centre of major importance.
Also in the Forum stood the Comitium, the voting-hall for elections to
public office, and the municipal
buildings assigned to the city's public
administration. Here too were the
Macellum or covered market for the
sale of provisions, the Building of Eu-

machia, the seat of the guild of cloth
dyers and bleachers, and a series of
warehouses, granaries, etc. A bustling
concourse of people from different
walks of life, and a lively aggregation
of different interests, characterized
this great square, which had in the
Capitolium, the site on which stood
the Temple of Jupiter, the very sym-
bol, the ideal heart, of Pompeii. At
one time, the Forum was completely
surrounded by a two-storeyed colonnade, its two superimposed orders -
the lower Doric, the upper Ionic - constructed at different periods. It was
ornamented with the statues of famous men and contained the tribune
of the orators. Let us now look in
more detail at the various buildings

The Basilica

This building, of the greatest elegance, has very large proportions: it
has a rectangular plan measuring 55 x

24 metres. Its imposing size is a measure of the importance it came to assume, since it was the main civic building assigned not only to the administration of justice - Pompeii's law-courts in fact - but also to the conducting of all public and private business and to the drawing up of economic contracts.

The building, divided into three aisles by a series of robust columns, is preceded by a portico and terminates in an elevated podium or tribunal for the presiding magistrate.

Thanks to the excavation of tiles, it has been possible to infer that the Basilica was entirely roofed-in. As far as its date of construction is concerned, this is somewhat uncertain, but the general consensus among scholars would date it to the 2nd century B.C.

THE TEMPLE OF APOLLO

Situated to the left of the Basilica, on the other side of the Via Marina, it is of very ancient origin, but was reconstructed in the mid-lst century A.D., the period in which its decoration was added. It consists of a huge arcaded court supported by columns with Corinthian capitals. Within this court was the cella (sanctuary) of the God preceded by a stairway and surrounded by columns. In front of the steps stands the sacrificial altar.

Standing against the columns of the portico are two fine bronze statues of Apollo and Diana, the originals of which are now preserved in the Archaeological Museum in Naples. We may also note the sun-dial placed on the Ionic column situated to the left of the steps.

Proceeding beyond the Temple of Apollo, along the side of the Forum, we may identify, to the left, the Mensa ponderaria, or office for the control of weights and measures; the Horrea or warehouses, probably for grain;

and, at the corner, the public latrines. At the end of the Forum, on its northern side, stands

THE TEMPLE OF JUPITER

Which rises proudly over a high flight of steps and is flanked by two honorary arches. The building, which occupies the Roman area of the Capitolium, the central nucleus of Pompeii, represents the religious heart of the city. Dating to the 2nd century B.C., it was seriously damaged by the earthquake in 62 A.D. and by the eruption of Vesuvius. Yet the remains visible today still testify to the grandeur and scale of its construction. It was preceded by an arcaded court which formed its atrium and of which only a few fluted columns survive. We now cross over to the other longitudinal - the eastern - side of the Forum. Here, flanking the right-hand side of the Temple of Jupiter, we are confronted by Macellum.

The Basilica.

THE MACELLUM

A large and important building, the Macellum was in fact the covered market of the town. It is rectangular in shape, and the various trading-stalls are distributed along its four sides, both on the outside and the inside. At the centre of its inner courtyard was a circular domed edicula. The walls of the building still preserve remains of its wonderful pictorial decoration. The building dates to the imperial period. Adjoining the Macellum is

above: statue of Apollo.
below: overall view of the Temple of Apollo.

THE TEMPLE OF THE LARES

A shrine built in honour of the Lares, the tutelary gods of the home, to commemorate the destruction of the town by the earthquake in 62 A.D.

Next to it, along the side of the Forum, is

THE TEMPLE OF VESPASIAN

Sacred to the cult of the emperor, little remains of this temple other than its basement and a fine marble altar with bas-relief decorations representing a sacrificial ceremony. Continuing along the eastern side of the Forum, we come next to

THE BUILDING OF EUMACHIA

Another building of considerable size, it served as the seat of the fullones: the fullers or dyers of cloth, a trade that acquired increasing economic importance in Pompeii, so much so as to have their premises on the central square of the town. Eumachia was the name of the priestess who acted as protectress of the guild in question and who sponsored the building's construction.

A two-storeyed colonnade precedes the entrance to the hall which consists of a magnificent portal decorated with marble bas-reliefs. This gives access to a hug courtyard surrounded by a fin colonnade and terminating in thre apses.

These contained statues of Eu machia and Livia, wife of the em peror Augustus. We come next to

THE COMITIUM

This building, situated at the corne of the Forum, was once used as voting-hall for the holding of elec tions.

The southern side of the Forum i closed by three buildings whic once served as the Municipal O fices.

Altar of the Temple of Vespasian.

Panoramic view of the remains of the Temple of Jupiter.
Building of Eumachia: aerial view of the whole.

Our departure point for this itinerary is the Forum, more precisely the right-hand side of the Temple of Jupiter/ From here we reach (to the left).

THE FORUM BATHS

The building is well-preserved, and clearly exemplifies the typical layout of Roman thermal complexes and the water-heating and cooling systems they used. It comprises a frigidarium (cold room), tepidarium (tepid room) and calidarium (hot room). Some of the other rooms served as dressing rooms or gymnasia. The women's section is carefully segregated from the men's. This bath-house complex dates to the 1st century B.C., more precisely to the 80s. On leaving the Forum Baths on the Via delle Terme, we come to one of the most beautiful and fasci-

nating of the houses of Pompeii, namely:

THE HOUSE OF THE TRAGIC POET

(ins. 8, n° 5)

This is a typical, luxurious dwelling of the affluent Pompeian bourgeoisie. It consists of numerous rooms and also two shops which testify to the commercial activity of the family. It is richly decorated, moreover, with frescoes and mosaics. Of the former, we should mention those in the triclinium depicting mythological scenes; now preserved in the Archaeological Museum in Naples, they represent one of the most significant groups of surviving wall paintings from antiquity. Of the mosaics, we may mention, in particular, the famous one of a dog with the inscription "cave canem" (beware of the dog), and also another one situated in the tablinum representing a choragus or theatrical director. It is this latter mosaic that has given the house its name.

Again on the Via delle Terme, to the side of the House of the Tragic Poet, is

THE HOUSE OF PANSA (ins. 6, n° 1)

A residence of such huge proportions that in the years immediately preceding the destruction of Pompeii it was subdivided into several apartments, each of them provided with its own personal entrance.

Dating back to the Samnite period the house originally belonged to single family. Its ancient decoration has completely disappeared.

We now turn into the Via Consolare and proceed along it until we come to an interesting baker's shop equipped with a large millstone for the milling of wheat. Just beyond is

THE HOUSE OF SALLUST (ins. 2, n° 4)

This represents one of the most significant examples of a house of the Samnite period, characterized by its decoration in stucco. Inside it has a large atrium of Tuscan type i.e. with the roof sloping inwards so as to allow the rainwater to run of into the central basin or cistern known as the impluvium.

The peristyle area has a plan and decoration of Roman type. The

Forum Baths.

ouse of the Tragic Poet: in the entrance is the well-known depiction of the "cave canem" (beware of the dog) in mosaic.
ouse of Pansa: overall view of the area of the peristyle.

paintings with a representation of the myth of Diana and Actaeon were unfortunately destroyed by bombardments in the Second World War.

We continue along the Via Consolare and, after passing the ancient warehouses for salt and the building which was the seat of the salt guild, we come to

THE HOUSE OF THE SURGEON

(ins. I, n° 9)

So-called because several surgical implements were found in it, of considerable interest for furthering our knowledge of ancient medical techniques. Fairly well-preserved and essentially unaltered in its original structure, this house represents a very fine example of an Italic house dating to the period between the 4th and 3rd century B.C.

A short distance beyond it, on the same street, we may visit the **HOUSE OF THE VESTALS**, of which

Villa of Diomedes.

the entrance area is particularly interesting, and, just beyond it,

THE PORTA ERCOLANO

or Herculanean Gate. This three-arched gateway is incorporated in Pompeii's circuit of walls, on its northwest corner. It was erected in Roman times on the site of a previous Samnite gate. The two lateral arches were reserved for pedestrians. Turning to the right of the Porta Ercolano we may follow the circuit of walls past Towers XII, XI and X to the Porta Vesuvio. Or we may take the road in front of the gate, namely the Via delle Tombe, and make our way to a huge cemetery and a series of suburban villas.

The Via delle Tombe (or Via dei Sepolcri as it is sometimes called) was brought to light during the excavations of Pompeii in the late 18th and early 19th century. The discovery immediately revealed itself as one of major importance, since this street and the whole complex of the Necropolis and its neighbouring villas constitute one of the most exhaustive and significant examples of a highly developed suburban area. It should further be emphasized that the tombs present a very wide range of architectural styles and a monumentality and refinement - especially in the case of the tombs of noble families - that are unmatched in other Roman cemeteries in the area. We may mention, in particular, the tombs of Cerrinius Restitutus, Aulus Veius, Marcus Porcius, the priestess Mamia, and the mausoleum of

the family of the Histacidi. Othe noteworthy tombs in the Necropo lis include the Tomb of the Gar lands, that of the Blue Vase, and th one in the form of an exedra. Alon the same street, we may then note a number of shops, followed b some houses and villas. The latte include the **VILLA OF THE MOSAI COLUMNS,** so-called because fou fine columns with interesting mosa ic decoration (currently housed i the Archaeological Museum i Naples) were found inside it.

Proceeding further along this stree we pass some other fine tombs such as that of Umbricius Scauru (with stucco decorations), Calven tius Quintus, and the Mausoleum c Histacidius Elenus erected by hi wife, and decorated with a bas-re lief representing funerary rites.

We now come to one of the larges and most beautiful of Pompeii's vil las:

THE VILLA OF DIOMEDES

This sumptuous dwelling, thoug retaining the salient features of th Pompeian house, is distinguishe by its proportions and, more espe cially, by the luminousness of it rooms. It is in fact planned in such way as to receive light both from in side and outside through large win dows and arcades, terraces and gai dens. Moreover, it is cleverly cor toured to the lie of the land, its va ious floor levels being staggered i such a way as to exploit th panoramic potentialities of the site The villa is arranged round a per style or atrium, with its variou rooms laid out around it. These ir clude a splendid apse-shaped bec room, lit by large windows and th complex of bathrooms with a sma pool. Beyond the tablinum and th triclinium, a loggia overlooks th large garden, access to which is pro vided by a stairway. This garder the largest in Pompeii, is equippe with a beautiful pool and a summe triclinium (dining room), and con pletely surrounded by an arcade. Eighteen victims of the eruption c Vesuvius - who had vainly soug refuge in a vaulted cellar - wer found during the excavations of th villa. Its decorations have large been lost. Not far from the Villa Diomedes, on the further outskii of Pompeii, we reach

Via dei Sepolcri.

THE VILLA OF THE MYSTERIES

Undoubtedly one of the most famous and beautiful of Pompeii's houses, not only due to its complex architectural plan, but also its wonderful decoration which represents one of the most interesting pictorial cycles surviving from antiquity.

The house was built in the 2nd century B.C., but was successively enlarged and transformed, gradually acquiring its existing proportions and plan. It lies on a slope facing the sea. To compensate for the sloping ground, the villa was built over a raised embankment to give it a level floor. Moreover, thanks to a series of porticoes, hanging gardens and terraces which connect the building with the surrounding area, an unusually striking and ingenious integration with the natural environment was achieved.

In essence, the villa has a rectangular plan. One enters through a beautiful and luminous exedra flanked by arcades and hanging gardens. This leads into the tablinum and the atrium. The former is notable for its beautiful decoration with tiny figures on a black ground. From a cubicle to the right of it, it too decorated with paintings, including the fine representation of a "Dancing Satyr", we pass into the famous "Room of the Dionysiac Mysteries", the room from whose wo[n]derful cycle of frescoes the nam[e] and the celebrity of this villa hav[e] been derived.

Before discussing these frescoes [in] more detail, let us first take a loo[k] at the rest of the villa. The patricia[n] living quarters were distribute[d] round the atrium, from which o[ne] passed into the peristyle with a t[u]fa colonnade. A small atrium adja[?] cent to it is striking for its fine pic[-] torial decoration. Lastly, we ma[y] identify the various ancillary room[s] assigned to the kitchens, the livin[g] quarters of the servants, and th[e] cellars and storerooms in whic[h] farm implements and the produc[e]

Villa of the Mysteries: view of the outside, constructed on staggered levels.

...ie frescos showing "the initiation into the Dionysiac rites".

the land were stored. It should be noted that the main entrance to the villa was situated on the opposite side to that of the exedra. Let us now go back to the "Room of the Dionysiac Mysteries" and say something about its pictorial "Cycle of the Mysteries", a pictorial complex that is truly exceptional both due to its scale - it entirely covers the walls of the room and all its figures are of life-size dimensions - and, more particularly, its extraordinary beauty. The narrative sequence of the frescoes flows freely from compartment to compartment. The individual episodes of the cycle succeed one another in logical sequence, which at the same time presents the temporal succession. The procession of figures finds its way along the walls, heightened in expression by the impact, earthy background of the beautiful Pompeian red against which they are set. The cycle as a whole is unique and incomparable in effect; the visitor is conscious of

being confronted by one of the greatest artistic expressions of the ancient world.

The author of these frescoes was an unknown Campanian painter of the 1st century B.C. Scholars are still not agreed on the interpretation of this cycle of paintings. But the most plausible hypothesis is that which sees in it a representation of the "Dionysiac Mysteries" and, more particularly, the rites of initiation of betrothed men and women in the cult of the god Dionysus. Though these rites had been prohibited by the Roman Senate, they continued to be practised by many families in secret, and this was especially the case in Southern Italy where this cult always had a great number of adepts. They probably included the family that owned this villa and in particular the mistress of the house, whom some scholars think is portrayed in the seated and veiled woman who observes the ceremony to one side.

Let us now look at the sequence of

scenes as identified according to the most reliable interpretation, starting from the wall to the north:

1st scene: a standing woman, who is about to be initiated in the cult, listens to the reading out of the formulae of the Dionysiac rite by a young boy, while another seated woman follows this phase of the ceremony;

2nd scene: an adolescent girl bears a platter with offerings towards a group of persons: the seated woman seen from the back awaits the ceremony of purification while the other two standing figures assist her;

3rd scene: a Silenus plays the lyre and a satyr the pan-pipes, while beside them a girl is milking a goat;

4th scene: a woman flees in terror;

5th scene: a Silenus holds out a wine bowl for a satyr to drink; another satyr holds a theatrical mask in his outstretched hand;

6th scene: the nuptials of Bacchus and Ariadne;

7th scene: a young woman uncovers

or protects with her hand the s[...] cred object, i.e. the mystic "van[...] us", the basket containing the sym[...] bol of fertility; beside her a winge[...] woman raises her arm and strike[...] with a whip - such was the ritu[...] prescribed for the adepts of D[...] onysus - the bared back of a woma[...] (the person about to be initiate[...] who kneels, resting her head on th[...] lap of a young female friend

-8th scene: the swirling dance of[...] bacchante gripped by the wild e[...] citement of the rite;

9th scene: the novice is prepare[...] for initiation helped by a fema[...] companion;

10th scene: a seated woman, pe[...] haps a portrait of the mistress[...] the Villa of the Mysteries, observ[...] the ceremony.

Left: *Silenus and Satyrs.*
Below: *Reading of the ritual.*
Opposite: *Silenus playing the lyre*

Scene of the flagellation - Detail.
Flagellation of a woman and dance of the Bacchante.

ung woman being flagellated.

Arch of Caligula.

Temple of Fortuna Augusta.

Our departure point is once again the Forum. Proceeding along the right side of the Temple of Jupiter and along the Via del Foro, we come to its intersection with the Via delle Terme and the Via della Fortuna. To the right before crossing it we see

THE TEMPLE OF FORTUNA AUGUSTA

a building erected in the year 3 B.C. at the behest of an important personage in the civic life of Pompeii, Marcus Tullius, who donated his own plot of ground for the purpose. Access to the temple is given by a flight of steps which includes a pla form on which the sacrificial alt rests. Over it rises the templ pronaos supported by handsor columns with Corinthian capita and, behind it, the cella (sanctuar with the aedicula and niches whi at one time contained statues.

After passing the **Arch of Caligul** we continue along the Via Mercuri A short distance further on, to th right, we come to

THE HOUSE OF THE ANCHOR

(ins. 10, n°

which preserves a beautiful garde surrounded by a series of niche and a colonnade. The house ow its name to the mosaic representir an anchor on its threshold.

Almost opposite, on the left, is shop for the washing and dyeing cloth, followed in turn by

THE HOUSE OF THE LARGE
FOUNTAIN (ins. 8, n° 22)

THE HOUSE OF THE SMALL
FOUNTAIN (ins. 8, n° 23)

Situated next to each other, th are so called because their garde are ornamented with splend fountains, one larger and one sma er, which are completely faced wi gaily coloured mosaics, patterne with delicate motifs. The decorati style is Egyptian in origin. In t first of these houses, copies of t bronze statues that once adorned are placed beside the fountain; the other, the walls are decorate with interesting naturalistic lan scape paintings.

A little further on, to the right, come to

THE HOUSE OF CASTOR
AND POLLUX (ins. 9, n° 6)

Consisting of three distir dwellings under the same roof, t house is notable for its marvello atrium surrounded by Corinthi columns. Interesting fresco de orations depicting mythologic scenes may be found in a room the right of the tablinum; oth

use of the Large Fountain - Nymphaeum in Mosaic.

paintings decorate the walls of the peristyle. The second peristyle with paintings of the 4th style is also very elegant.

On the left of the Via Mercurio we come next to

THE HOUSE OF ADONIS (ins. 7, n° 18)

This house contains, on one of the walls of its garden, one of the best known and most interesting of the paintings found at Pompeii. It is a fresco of "Adonis wounded, tended by Venus". In an adjoining room, other paintings depicting a Hermaphrodite may be seen.

Almost opposite, on the right side of the Via Mercurio is the **HOUSE OF THE CENTAUR** and, just beyond it,

THE HOUSE OF MELEAGER (ins. 9, n° 2)

This interesting house dates back to the Samnite period, but it was reconstructed and decorated in a lat-er period, as testified by the remains of paintings visible in some of its rooms. The house is equipped with an elegant reception room or parlour, enclosed on three sides by beautiful Corinthian columns. Particularly pleasing for its harmonious and graceful plan is the peristyle which has at its centre a large basin decorated by sculptures and surrounded by a colonnade.

The Via Mercurio ends at the circuit of walls surrounding the town, in the stretch between the Porta Ercolano and the Porta Vesuvio. It is here fortified by three towers, identified as Towers XII, XI and X; Tower XI - at the end of the Via Mercurio - is also called the Tower of Mercury and was built over the remains of an ancient Pompeian gate. Parts of the more ancient fortifications bearing inscriptions in the Oscan tongue can be identified along this stretch of the walls. An ascent of the tower is recommended, since it com-mands extensive panoramic view of much of the excavations and the majestic backdrop of Vesuviu which now looms calmly ar serenely over the city it once de stroyed.

Following the circuit of the walls the right, we reach the nearby Por Vesuvio, one of the main gatewa leading into Pompeii. Close to it w may see the aqueduct whic brought water into the town, whi just beyond it are a number tombs of local personages.

We now turn into the Via Vesuv and proceed along it as far as its i tersection with the Vicolo Mercuri Here we find

THE HOUSE OF THE GILDED CUPID

(ins. 16, n°

In its architectural layout and dec ration it is one of the most refine and aristocratic of the houses Pompeii. It belonged to a rich fam ly of probably patrician origin, as a tested by the name of its owne Gnaius Poppaeus Atticus. The irre ularity of the ground, combine with a taste for new, original ar even scenic interior designs, led the creation of a peristyle which raised on one side, almost creati the effect of a theatrical stage. Tf impression is also reinforced by tf numerous masks that constitute tf recurrent motif of the decoration the panels between the columns the arcade. A small room of the ari tocratic living quarters is adorne with a magnificent decoration gilded cupids in small round fielc from which the house takes i name. Other paintings decorate tf walls and ceilings of other room they include those of "Diana ai Actaeon", "Leda" and "Venus fis ing" situated in a room adjacent the triclinium, and those depicti various mythological figures on tf walls of the triclinium itself. Al noteworthy is the fine floor by tf entrance, decorated with mytholc ical scenes of "Leda with the swa and "Narcissus looking at his refle tion in the fountain". Overall, t decoration of this house is partic larly refined and thought out in t most minute detail. It reveals artistic taste which strives after pi ciosity and scenic effect. Continui along the Vicolo Mercurio, we cor to the famous House of the Vetti

House of the Gilded Cupids: the name derives from the depiction of golden Cupids situated in one of the cubicula.

ouse of the Gilded Cupids.
ouse of the Gilded Cupids - Peristyle.

HOUSE OF THE VETTII (ins. 15, n° 1)

A splendid and excellently preserved patrician residence, the House of the Vettii represents the most striking example of the dwelling of a family that won prestige and importance in the town thanks to the practise of trade and hence the accumulation of wealth. The striving after luxury, the conspicuous display of beautiful and precious objects, and the attention lavished on the decoration of every corner of the house, all reveal the concern of its owners - who were two brothers, Aulus Vettius Restitutus and Aulus Vettius Conviva - to forget their humble origins and assimilate themselves into the aristocratic class of the town, thus turning their splendid residence into a means of social promotion. It is not by chance that it is completely devoid of the shops which, in antiquity, were normally so closely linked with the houses of merchants.

Let us now take a more detailed look at its various rooms and, more especially, the wonderful decoration that characterizes it and that represents one of the finest and most comprehensive examples of the ornamental style known as "painting of the 4th style" with its rich ornamentation with tiny figural scenes, floral motifs, friezes and playful cupids.

On entering the house, we find in its Vestibule a representation of Priapus, emblem of fertility, placed here to banish envy. We then pass into the Atrium, where we may note two strong-boxes and a fine decoration with "Cupids and Psyche".

We then enter the room to the left of the entrance, which is decorated with paintings of "Ariadne abandoned" and "Hero and Leander", as well as a frieze with a beautiful fish motif. The following room is decorated with wall paintings of other mythological figures and episodes from their lives. We then pass into the atrium, which opens out into two recesses, decorated with two charming murals: one representing a "Cock Fight", and the other portraying "Medusa" and "Silenus".

We pass into the adjacent peristyle, an elegant open court embellished with a beautiful colonnade and a number of statuettes which serve as little fountains.

The Triclinium (dining room), situated to the right of the peristyle, is a splendid room adorned with the magnificent pictorial decoration already referred to above. The room is truly evocative and the paintings create a unique atmosphere, representing at the same time one of the most significant testimonies of the art of the period. The walls of the room are completely painted in red and divided into compartments by black bands. A long frieze running right round the walls represents a series of "Cupids" intent on variou activities and forms of trade. Beginning from the right we see: Cupid throwing stones at a target; Cupid weaving garlands; Cupids manufacturing and selling perfumes; Cupid engaged in chariot-racing; Cupid making wine; Cupids at the feast of Bacchus; and Cupids selling wine.

In the lower part of the walls, at the level of the candelabra, are similar bands, some of which are depicted with scenes of "Psyche" gathering flowers. Apart from these ornamental friezes, the room is decorated with three large wall painting "Agamemnon intent on killing the sacred hind", "Apollo after vanquishing the Python" and "Orestes and Pylades in the presence of Thoas and Iphigenia".

Other smaller paintings with mythological subjects, celebrating famous couples, such as "Apollo and Daphne", "Bacchus and Ariadne" "Perseus and Andromeda" and "Poseidon and Amymone", may also be found in the same room.

The House of the Vettii contain still further wall paintings in other rooms in the north-eastern area. One of them is decorated with large wall-panels painted with mythological scenes and, above them, a large and elaborate frieze consisting of ornamental motifs and architectural perspectives. Similar decoration may be found in a room in the south-eastern area of the house.

Charming, too, is the gynaeceum. And lastly the kitchens enable one to catch a fascinating glimpse of the domestic life of the past.

On leaving the House of the Vettii on the same little street, the Vico Mercurio, we find

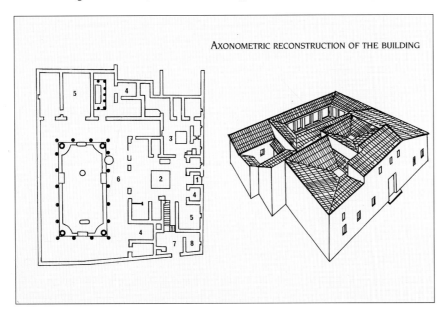

AXONOMETRIC RECONSTRUCTION OF THE BUILDING

1 - Entrance
2 - Atrium
3 - Small Atrium with Lararium
4 - Cubiculum
5 - Oecus
6 - Peristyle
7 - Entrance to service area
8 - Stable for building

A delightful corner of the House of the Vettii.

Cupids as vintners.

Cupids as goldsmiths.

ercules strangling the serpent.

THE HOUSE OF THE LABYRINTH

(ins. 11, n°

Dating to the Samnite period. I takes its name from the mosaic i one of its rooms representing th myth of Theseus and Ariadne an the Labyrinth. Some of the room are finely decorated with architec tural motifs of the 2nd style. W may also note the interesting re ception rooms, the presence of th double atrium, and the bakehous and bathroom incorporated in th left half of the house. We continu along the Vicolo Mercurio, and the turn left into the Via del Fauno i the direction of the Via della Fortu na. This brings us to

Above: *House of the Labyrinth.*
Below: *the House of the Fau panoramic glimpse of the atrium wher the bronze statue of the Faun stands.*

THE HOUSE OF THE FAUN

(ins. 12, n° 2-5)

Undoubtedly one of the most beautiful and sumptuous, and also one of the largest, of Pompeii's houses. It derives its name from the statuette of the Faun that stands in the impluvium, a charming sculpture in bronze whose original is now housed in the Archaeological Museum in Naples. The wonderful mosaics that once adorned this house the best known is the one representing the "Battle of Alexander" - have also been transferred to the museum. But many of the rooms still retain important decorations, including the peristyle which is enriched with interesting works in stucco, 28 Ionic columns and an exedra. To the back of the house is a larger peristyle with a garden. The fine mosaic floors that decorate many of the rooms should also be noted.

The dancing Faun: one of the most valuable examples of Pompeian statuary.

We again leave the Forum by the Via del Foro to the right of the Temple of Jupiter, and then turn right into the Via della Fortuna and its continuation the Via di Nola until we come to the Quadrivium (or crossroads) of Orpheus. Here we turn left into the Via Vesuvio. On the left, we may visit the **HOUSE OF ORPHEUS** (ins. 14, n° 20), noteworthy for its painting of "Orpheus among the wild beasts". Just beyond it is a Dyer's Shop (n° 22) and a Gambling Den (n° 28), which served not only as a gaming house but also as a brothel. To the right of the same street is the **HOUSE OF CAECiLiUS JUCUNDUS** (ins. 1, n° 26), a prominent Pompeian banker as is corroborated by the finding of his account books and strong-box. His house is undoubtedly one of the finest and richest in the town, as was consonant with its owner's social status. It contains some wonderful remains of wall paintings and a bronze portrait bust of the banker. Next to it, on the Via di Nola, is the **HOUSE OF THE BULLOCK** (Casa del Torello) (ins. 1, n° 7), which contains a fine nymphaeum. Just beyond it on the Via di Nola is the **HOUSE OF QUEEN MARGHERiTA** (ins. 2, n° 1) with remains of paintings of mythological scenes. We now make a detour to the left to the Via dell Nozze d'Argento, where we find th

HOUSE OF THE SILVER WEDDING

(Casa delle Nozze d'Argento) (ins. 2 One of the richest and most spler didly patrician in the town. It wa excavated on the occasion of th silver wedding of King Umberto (hence its name).

Samnite in origin but remodelle in Roman times, the house has large atrium supported by ta Corinthian columns. Of great effec is the room characterized by a bar rel-vaulted ceiling resting on fou columns painted in imitation c marble. The decorations with whic

House of the Silver Wedding - Perystyle.
Opposite: *House of Marcus Lucretius.*

e walls of many of the rooms are ainted are also of great distinction. The house was also provided ith its own private bath-house omprising a calidarium, tepidarim and frigidarium (hot, tepid and old water rooms).

e now turn back as far as the uadrivium of Orpheus. On the ght, at the beginning of the Via di ola, we find

HE CENTRAL BATHS

his extensive bath-house complex ccupies an entire insula (block). It as built after the earthquake in 62 .D. to satisfy the growing needs of e citizens of Pompeii which the orum Baths were now inadequate cope with. The Central Baths ere in fact constructed on imroved criteria, and equipped not nly with a palaestra (gymnasium), ut also with a sudatio, or sauna situated in a large chamber with a omed roof.

short distance beyond, on the Via tabiana, is

HE HOUSE OF MARCUS LUCRETIUS

(ins. 3, n° 5)

his was the house of an illustrious erson in Pompeii, the priest of the od Mars.

its rear is a charming small terced garden which is laid out at a igher level than the rest of the ouse. It is ornamented with a number of marble statuettes, creating a onderful effect.

ome of the rooms, such as the atrim and the little rooms round it, ill preserve some of their murals, ut the most interesting of the wall aintings have been transferred to e Archaeological Museum in aples. On returning to the Central aths, we now continue along the ia di Nola. This street constituted e decumanus of the town, i.e. the rincipal thoroughfare intersecting ompeii from west to east. The caro maximus, the street running at ght angles to it and hence from orth to south, consisted of the Via esuvio - Via Stabiana thoroughre. We now come, on the right, to

HE HOUSE OF THE CENTENARY

(ins. 8, n° 3)

takes its name from the 18th Cennary of the eruption of Vesuvius, e year in which it was excavated.

It is a house with a complex plan, since it results from a fusion of more than one dwelling. Some of its rooms are notable both in structure and decoration. It was here that the charming bronze statuette of a "Satyr with wine skin" was found. One of the two atriums is paved with a fine mosaic floor. Two rooms to the side of the peristyle are painted in white and black, while others are frescoed with mythological subjects. Continuing our itinerary, we may make a detour to the left into the Vicolo di Lucrezio to visit the **HOUSE OF MARCUS LUCRETIUS FRONTO** (ins. 4, n° 10), a small but elegant and well-proportioned house of the Roman period.

Noteworthy is the decoration of its rooms with a series of mythological paintings. On returning to the Via di Nola, we come, on the left, to the **HOUSE OF THE GLADIATORS** (ins. 5, n° 3) which served as the dwelling of the families of circus gladiators. A little further on, to the left of the Via di Nola, is the **HOUSE OF OBELLIUS FIRMUS**, a noble and decorous building of the Samnite period. The paintings that decorate it are of some interest. On reaching the end of the street, we come to the Porta di Nola, a town gate dating to the Samnite period and characterized by a single arch. A cemetery has been discovered beyond the gate.

V ITINERARY

The quarters to the East of the Forum (Region VII)

We take the Via del Foro to the right of the Temple of Jupiter until we come to the Temple of Fortuna Augusta. From here begins an extensive quarter which in fact constitutes the oldest nucleus of Pompeii. It is densely packed with houses, big and small; and the streets that intersect it are not always regular in plan. A visit to this district is thus especially interesting and evocative because it gives us an exceptionally vivid picture of the most heavily urbanized part of the town. Adjacent to the Temple of Fortuna Augusta, on the Via Fortuna, we find the **HOUSE OF THE BLACK WALL** (Casa della Parete Nera) (ins. 4, n° 59) which derives its name from the decoration in

black of one of its rooms. The house is noble and elegant in appearance. Immediately after it is the **HOUSE OF THE FIGURED CAPITALS** (ins. 4, n° 57), it too of noble appearance. It is characterized by an interesting entrance-hall flanked by pillars surmounted by sculpted capitals (these are now displayed in the Antiquarium).

Just beyond it, on the same side of the street, is the **HOUSE OF ARIADNE or OF THE COLOURED CAPITALS** (ins. 4, n° 51): its takes its alternative name from the series of polychrome capitals at its entrance. Some of the paintings that decorate the rooms are also interesting. Adjacent to it is the **HOUSE OF THE HUNT** (Casa della Caccia) (ins. 4, n° 58), characterized by a number of wall paintings with a variety of subject-matter; some of them depicting mythological episodes, others landscapes or scenes of hunting.

At this point of our itinerary a detour is recommended by the Vicolo

Storto, a narrow curving stree where, in the midst of densel built-up houses, we find the **BAK ERY OF MODESTUS,** a completel equipped bakehouse with its over mill-stone, storerooms for flour, an counters for the conservation an sale of bread. The ordinary, ever day life of Pompeii is revived these perfectly preserved remain the past lives on unchanged in a its evocativeness and simplicit They are aspects of the daily life c Pompeii which, by a strange de tiny, the tragedy of the eruption c Vesuvius, have been permitted t survive unaltered.

If we wish, we can make another de tour along the Via del Panettier Modesto to the **HOUSE OF GAVIU RUFUS** (ins. 2, n° 16) and othe houses. Returning to the Vicol Storto, we continue down it until w come to its intersection with the Vi degli Augustali, which begins fror the northern end of the Forum. Ha way along it, on the left, stands th

Mil and Oven.

...abian Baths.

OUSE OF THE BEAR (Casa del-
Orso) (ins. 2, no 45) with a charm-
g fountain in its inner garden.
e now take the street that forms
e continuation of the Vicolo Stor-
, namely the Vicolo di Eumachia,
ntinuing down it as far its inter-
ction with the Vicolo del Balcone
nsile. Here, on the corner, is an
cient **HOTEL** and, adjacent to it,
e **HOUSE WITH THE BALCONY**
° 28), characterized by a graceful
ojecting balcony which is perhaps
e first example of its kind in the
wn.
oceeding along the same narrow
reet, after passing one or two tav-
ns, we come, on the left, to the
JPANARE or brothel (ins. 1, n°
): the purpose of this house is
mply demonstrated by the layout
its rooms (on two floors) and the
scene or erotic paintings and
affiti with which they are decorat-
. Facing it is the **HOTEL OF SIT-
US** (Hospitium Sittii) (ins. 1, n°.
) and nearby the **HOUSE OF SIR-**

ICUS (ins. 1, n° 47), which consists
of two intercommunicating dwellings, one of which has its entrance
on the Via Stabiana. The house contains some valuable paintings and a
series of handsome rooms which at-
test to the affluence of its owners.
Turning right into the Vicolo del Lupanare, we come to

THE STABIAN BATHS

This is a fascinating and complete-
ly-equipped bathhouse complex
dating to successive periods, as attested by the varied structure and
decoration of its component parts.
The original nucleus of the complex
is the one on its northern side; this
dates to the Roman Republic (2nd
century B.C.), whereas much of the
decoration and various restorations
and extensions date to the early
imperial period.
The whole complex underwent a
major restoration in the years immediately following the earthquake
in 62 A.D. The Baths consist of three

parts, laid out on three of the four
sides of its inner courtyard: 1) the
block to the east comprises the
public baths divided into two sections, one for men and one for
women. They each comprise the
following rooms: a vestibule, dressing room, frigidarium (cold room),
tepidarium (tepid room) and calidarium (hot-room). Of considerable interest is the decoration in
stucco. 2) The group of premises to
the north comprises a large com-
mon latrine and a series of private
baths. As already mentioned, this is
the oldest part of the thermal complex, and access to it was given
from the Vicolo del Lupanare. 3)
The third section is the most modern one, not only in construction,
but also in functionality. It adopts
the criterion of the public bath
linked to the palaestra and hence
to gymnastic exercises. It is in fact
equipped with a large outdoor
swimming pool and areas and facilities for the practice of sports.

This itinerary is devoted in particular to the Triangular Forum and the complex of the Theatres of Pompeii: an area no less full of public buildings than the Forum and hence by no means a secondary focus of the political, social and religious life of the town.

We begin by taking the Via dell'Abbondanza (itself the subject of the following itinerary) which starts from between the Comitium and the Building of Eumachia at the southern end of the Forum. Turning right into the Vicolo dei Dodici Dei we come to the **HOUSE OF THE BOAR HUNT** (Casa del Cinghiale) (ins. 3, n° 8), so called on account of the subject-matter of a mosaic situated in its entrance passage.

It also preserves a fine mosaic decoration in its atrium, characterized by geometric designs.

We return to the Via dell'Abbondanza and take the next turning to the right into the Via dei Teatri which constitutes the main road of approach to the area of

THE TRIANGULAR FORUM

This whole area extends over a lava platform overlooking the plain below. It has assumed a triangular shape to conform to the natural lie of the land and thus to exploit the available space in the most efficient way.

The apex of the triangle is situated to the north and here we also find the entrance formed by the Propilaeum, a prospect of 6 Ionic columns (flanked by a public fountain). On crossing through this, we find ourselves faced by the extensive sacred area of the Triangular Forum, bounded by a long portico consisting of 95 Doric columns of great effect. The general layout of this Forum is mainly Hellenistic.

On entering it, we may note the marble pedestal that once supported a statue of Claudius Marcellus. Facing it, at the further end of the Forum, stand the remains of the **DORIC TEMPLE**, a noble building of considerable antiquity, dating back to the 6th century B.C., i.e. to the period when the whole surrounding area was under the direct influence of the Greeks. Of the original temple - in the ancient Greek style - only the basement preceded by a flight of steps and some fragmentary columns remain. At some points the transformations undergone by the temple in subsequent periods are visible: for example, the sanctuary placed to the side of the steps. The well to the rear and the sun-dial date to the Roman period. But the three tufa altars are pre-Roman in date.

Let us now proceed to visit the other buildings in the area. Firstly, on

Triangular Forum

emple of Isis.

he Via del Tempio di Iside, we
ome to

HE SAMNITE PALAESTRA

lso known as the Small Palaestra
o distinguish it from the large one
tuated close to the Amphitheatre
f the town). Very simple in struc-
re and quite small in size, it was

Pompeii's best known and most
popular centre for the practice of
gymnastics. It is rectangular in
shape and surrounded by a colonnade. The marble pedestal situated at the foot of one of the columns
once supported the famous statue
of the "Doryphoros" (now displayed
in the Archaeological Museum in

Naples), a splendid copy of the
Greek original by Polykleitos.
Adjacent to it, on the same street, is

THE TEMPLE OF ISIS

This is in fact the best preserved of
Pompeii's religious buildings and
also one whose decoration has remained virtually intact (though this

has now been transferred to the Archaeological Museum in Naples). It represents, moreover, one of the finest surviving temples of Greek type.

The sanctuary (cella) of the god stands high up on a basement and is surrounded by the aedicula which, on one side, opens out into a pronaos. The temple complex also comprises a shrine embellished with stuccoes, a subterranean cistern in which the water for sacrifices and ritual ablutions was kept, and a large room in which adepts of the cult of Isis held their meetings.

Alongside it stands

THE TEMPLE OF JUPITER MEILICHIOS

This is a small temple characterized by a fine altar in tufa. The terracotta statues of Jupiter, Juno and Minerva found here are now in the Museum in Naples.

Passing through the eastern portico of the Triangular Forum we come to

THE LARGE THEATRE

A magnificent building of Greek type with the **cavea**, i.e. the tiered seats, laid out in a natural cavity of the ground. It dates to the 2nd century B.C., but was restored and enlarged under the emperor Augustus, enabling it to accommodate up to 5000 spectators.

Of the **cavea** only the lower tiers remain. On the occasion of the performances staged in the theatre today during the summer theatrical season, the missing ones are substituted by wooden benches.

At one time the tiered seats could be protected from the rain, or the heat of the summer, by an awning supported by poles affixed to the summit of the outer wall.

The narrow stage is backed by a posterior wall formed by niches.

In front of it is the orchestra.

To one side of the Large Theatre stands

THE SMALL THEATRE

Graceful and harmonious, this small theatre was roofed and intended for musical performances. It could contain up to 1000 spectators.

Erected in the 1st century B.C., it constituted one of the finest examples of this genre of architecture.

To the rear of the Large Theatre (i.e. behind its stage) stands another imposing building:

THE BARRACKS FOR GLADIATORS

At one time this colonnaded court was reserved for the actors and also for the spectators, who could rest here during the intervals of the theatrical performances. But during the imperial period it was remodelled as a barracks for gladiators.

The building consists of a large rectangular arcaded court, surrounded by various living quarters for the gladiators and their families. The open area in the centre of the colonnade was used as an exercise yard. Numerous weapons and pieces of armour of the period were discovered in the barracks; now displayed in the Archaeological Museum of Naples, they provide invaluable evidence about the nature of gladiatorial combat.

Our way out brings us onto the Via Stabiana. Following this street, we may reach the **PORTA DI STABIA** at its end. This is in fact the most ancient of Pompeii's city gates, and occupies a position of great suggestiveness. It is incorporated in the ancient city walls and beyond it lies an area of tombs.

Aerial view of the Large Theatre, little Theatre and Gladiators' Barracks.

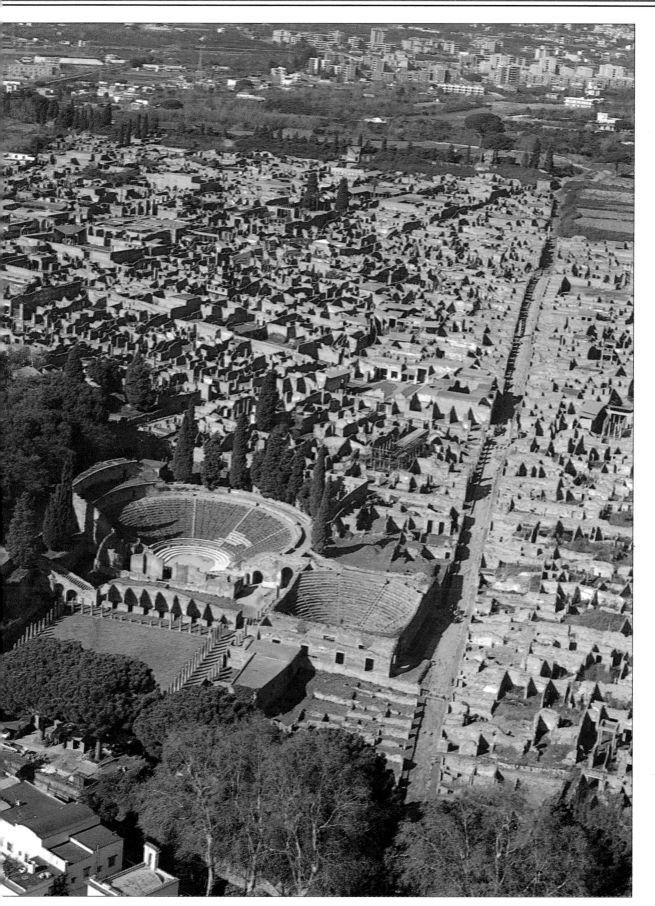

VII ITINERARY

From the Forum to the porta di Sarno; the via dell'Abbondanza; the Amphitheatre and the Palaestra; the porta Nocera

Pompeii has a typically Roman urbanistic layout, with the streets cutting each other at right angles and intersecting the city's main thoroughfares represented by the **Cardo** (the Via di Nola) and the **Decumanus** (the Via di Stabia). It was along these road arteries of major importance that the great houses and villas of the noble families had arisen, as well as some belonging to the newly emerging class of the rich bourgeoisie that had tried to emulate, if not surpass, in the sumptuousness of their residences, the patrician class that had long held power. Yet the progressive emergence

and ever more decisive self-affirmation of the new social class, combined with the great economic development of the town, also determined a change in Pompeii's urban pattern. It was thus that, with the passage of time, the centre of business and the new and flourishing civic nucleus came to be transferred to another major thoroughfare: this was the Via dell'Abbondanza. This street, which starts out from the Forum and cuts through the town from west to east to the Porta di Sarno, emerged as the commercial and business heart of the town and, as the expression

of the mercantile class that now guided the economic destiny o Pompeii, came to supplant the an cient **cardo** and **decumanus** in importance. The first stretch of the Via dell'Abbondanza traverse Pompeii's old city centre and the zone of the old excavations. It i then prolonged through a new area which also corresponds to the nev sector of the excavations. The se latter differ from previous excava tions because they are conceived in a fundamentally different way: the are aimed not at dismantling the finds, and transferring them to vari ous museums, but leaving them in tact *in situ*, including the paintings statues and furnishings that form an integral part of the buildings re covered. The purpose of this is to provide as comprehensive a pic ture as possible of the daily life in ancient Pompeii, and to permit wider and more realistic view of al the finds in their original position Moreover, where a need has arisen attempts have been made to recon struct the architectural parts tha are lacking in order to make the im age of Pompeii as it once was more vivid and to ensure that all the ar chaeological finds acquire a differ ent dimension and a role not a self-sufficient objects, but as inte gral parts of an overall view of the day-to-day life of the town.
The Via dell'Abbondanza is charac terized by a series of houses and shops stretching right along it course. The architectural structure of the houses is generally more complex: two-storey buildings are not uncommon, comprising the shop and storerooms on the groun floor and the living quarters and kitchens on the first floor. Balconie and galleries, and various system for exploiting the available space both internally and externally, are frequent feature. All this was natu rally dictated by the various re quirements of the mercantile and industrial class of the town who had to organize the available space in different way to enable them to practise their trade as commodi ously as possible. But it was also dictated by the enormous demo graphic growth of Pompeii, which was the consequence of economi development, and which required more functional, or at any rate dif ferent, organization of floor space. Let us now take a more detailed look at the buildings along thi street. Starting out from the Forur

Detail of the head and horn of plenty on the Fountain of Abundance.

to the side of the Building of Eumachia), we make our way along it towards the major intersection represented by the Quadrivium of Olonius. But before reaching this, we find to the right the **HOUSE OF CORNELIUS RUFUS** (ins. 4, n° 5), the dwelling of a noble family of Roman origin that is fairly elegant both in structure and decoration. Facing it across the street are the Stabian Baths which we have already had occasion to visit.

On passing the aforementioned Ouadrivium (crossroads), we see to the left the **HOUSE OF EPIDIUS RUFUS** (ins. 1, n° 22), characterized by a large and handsome atrium surrounded by elegant columns. Next to it is the **HOUSE OF EPIDIUS SABINUS** (ins. I, n° 22) which is in fact the result of the fusion of more than one building.

On the opposite side of the street is

THE HOUSE OF THE LYRE-PLAYER

(Casa del Citarista)   (ins. 4, n° 5, n. 25)

This unusually large house has one of its three entrances on the Via dell'Abbondanza. It is composite in structure, in that it results from the combination of two houses, of which the older one is situated on the ground floor and communicates with the Via Stabiana. The beautiful wall paintings that decorated this house are now preserved in the Archaeological Museum of Naples; as also is the famous bronze statuette of "Apollo the Lyre-Player" from which the house derives its name. Other notable bronze sculptures or-

ia dell'Abbondanza.

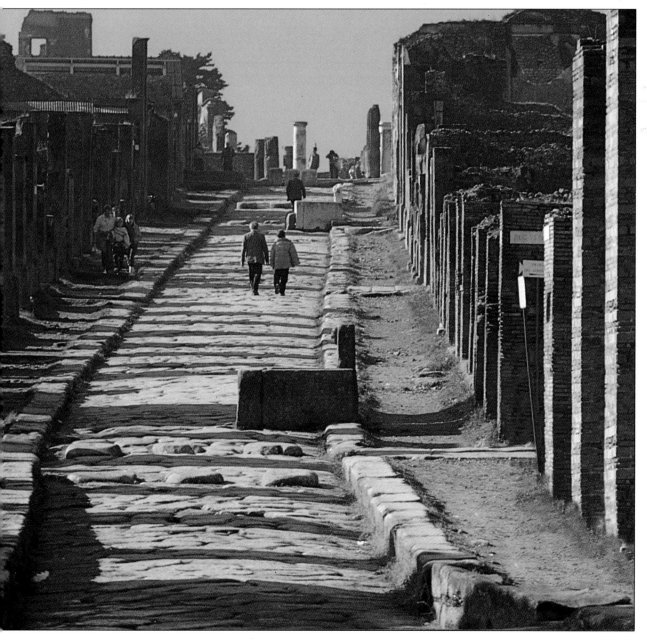

Fullonica Stephani.

namented the peristyle: mainly animal groups including the very famous one of the "Wild Boar attacked by Hounds". It is at this point that the zone commonly called that of the "New Excavations" begins. We may observe first of all some inscriptions placed on the façades of houses: they are in fact inscriptions of electoral propaganda. We then see on the left two shops, perhaps the property of one Popidius Montanus, of particular interest for their door-locking system. Next we come to the famous **WORKSHOP OF VERECUNDUS** (n° 7-5), a typical and well-preserved example of a shop for weavers and sales outlet for cloth. It is recognisable by its projecting porch roof and by the paintings that decorate its walls. They include representations of "Mercury", "Venus on a quadriga", "The weavers' workshops" and "The sale of cloth". All these are depicted with extreme freshness. The fact, moreover, that the paintings should have as their subject the actual activities performed in this workshop constitutes

a kind of advertisement of the shop and this makes it an historical document of considerable interest. Two other workshops are to be found just after that of Verecundus, one characterized by a balcony and a boiler in which the fabrics were placed to be dyed, and the other with a fine sculptural decorative frieze running along its balcony representing the gods.

On the right of the Via dell'Abbondanza we find the **HOUSE OF CASCA LONGUS,** noteworthy for the decoration of the ceiling and walls of its atrium with floral and theatrical motifs. Adjacent to it is

THE FULLER'S WORKSHOP OF STEPHANUS (n° 7)

Perhaps the most complete and interesting workshop for the dyeing and washing of cloth to survive in Pompeii; annexed to it is the home of its owner. The actual workshop was situated on the ground floor: here it is still possible to see the vat for the washing of the cloth, the basins for scouring it, the stands for treading it and the terrace for hang-

ing it out. On the upper floor are th living quarters. This building there fore represents a particularly clea example of the transformation un dergone by Roman domestic archi tecture in order to adapt itself t the new needs of the middle clas which had to find new space for th pursuit of its commercial and indus trial activities.

Adjacent to the Fuller's Workshop i

THE HOUSE OF THE LARARIUM

(ins. 6, n°

Although, at the time of the erup tion of Vesuvius, the reconstructio and decoration of this house ha not been completed, it is nonethe less possible to admire a fine serie of bas-reliefs, situated in particula in the Lararium. These consist of series of figural scenes in stucc against a blue ground, depictin episodes and scenes of life de scribed in the last canto of Homer Iliad: "Hector taking his leave of th Trojans and going off to fight agains Achilles"; "Hector is killed and h body dragged under the walls c roy"; "Hector's father, Priam, begs Achilles to restore his son's body to him, and then returns home".

This is followed by the **SHOP OF TERUS** (n° 3) in which vases and bronze implements were sold, and then by

THE HOUSE OF THE CRYPTOPORTICUS (n° 2)

localled on account of its cellars - or cryptoporticus - which, though in part transformed into a deposit for wine, still retains part of its original decoration consisting of a fine frieze and a series of mural panels depicting episodes of the Iliad. Very evocative for the light effects created by its narrow windows, this underground chamber also contains several "casts" of inhabitants of the house who thought they could escape from the eruption of Vesuvius by seeking refuge here, but who were suffocated to death by the exhalations of gas. Another fine decoration may be found in the **triclinium.** In an adjacent alley, we may also visit the **HOUSE OF LUCIUS CAIUS SECUN-**

DUS (ins. 6, n° 15). This is notable for its beautiful façade articulated with stucco decorations. Particularly graceful is the small atrium and also the internal stairway which led to the upper floor. Beyond the Vicolo Meridionale is another large and magnificent house:

THE HOUSE OF MENANDER

(ins. 10, n° 4)

It derives its name from the portrait of the poet Menander found on one of the walls of the house, but it owes its fame to the beauty and nobility of its rooms, and to the extraordinarily rich collection of silverware found in its cellars; this represents without a doubt one of the most significant treasures of antiquity. The architecture of some of its rooms, such as the peristyle, the triclinium, the atrium and the bathroom, is of considerable distinction. But it is the pictorial decoration of much of the rooms that is especially beautiful. Paintings depicting episodes of

the Trojan War are to be found in the **Lararium.** In two rooms opened up under the portico of the peristyle we may admire friezes representing the Centaurs and the Leucippides, while hunting scenes and theatrical figures, including the aforementioned portrait of Menander, decorate the walls of the exedrae. Particularly well preserved is the area of the baths and of the various domestic services including the kitchens, storerooms, cellars, stables and servants' quarters. Proceeding along a little street to the back of the House of Menander, we may visit

THE HOUSE OF THE LOVERS (n° 11)

(Casa degli Amanti)
A graceful and elegant house with the rooms arranged on two floors and almost all of them well-structured and harmoniously decorated. Our visit to the houses situated along the Via dell'Abbondanza now continues with

House of Menander.

THE HOUSE OF PAQUIUS PROCULUS

(ins. 7, n° 1)

In structure, it reveals a number of successive enlargements. The various rooms are noteworthy for their fine decoration. We may note for example the beautiful vestibule, dominated by an interesting complex of mosaics of animal subjects incorporated in a harmonious geometric frame: the whole of great effect. Noteworthy, too, is the well-proportioned peristyle, harmonious in form, airy and luminous in its sense of spaciousness.

A number of skeletons of children who died during the eruption of Vesuvius were also found in this house.

We come next to the small but graceful **HOUSE OF FABIUS AMANDIUS** (ins. 7, n° 2) and, just beyond it,

THE HOUSE OF THE PRIEST AMANDUS (ins. 7, n° 7)

On entering the house, just inside which are the remains of a human "cast" - another of the victims of Vesuvius - we may also note the mural painting that decorates the entrance wall; it represents "scenes of combat". Particularly fine is the **triclinium** with a series of mural panels of mythological subjects: "Ulysses on the ship", "Perseus and Andromeda", "Hercules in the Gardens of the Hesperides", and "Daedalus and Icarus". The charming garden of the peristyle with the "cast" of a tree is also interesting.

Turning into the little side street that follows on the right we come to

THE HOUSE OF THE EPHEBE

(ins. 7, n° 10)

So-called on account of the statue of an "Ephebe" found here and now displayed in the Archaeological Museum of Naples. Numerous bronze and terracotta objects and statuettes were also found here. The house was formed by the fusion of several dwellings. That it belonged to a very affluent family is clearly revealed by its conspicuous luxuriousness and sumptuous decoration. We may note its richly decorated rooms with their fine marble inlaid floors. In the bedrooms even the "casts" of the beds are visible. A fresco depicting "Venus and Mars" is situated in the garden.

Other paintings with scenes referring to ancient Egypt are visible in the **triclinium** which is situated in the open, but protected by a pergola.

Another house of more modest dimensions is linked with the House of the Ephebe: it has a fine peri

House of the Priest Amandus.
Niche in the House of the Ephebe.

...yle with painted walls. Its **ablinum** too is decorated with ...ural panels depicting the "Nup...als of Venus and Mars".

...ot far from this house is the **Dyer's hop** (n°19),on the Vicolo dell'E...bo which still preserves its basins ...r the washing of the cloth, its boil...s, amphorae and a graceful porti...

...e now return to the Via dell'Ab...ondanza where we may admire, on ...e left,

THE THERMOPOLION OF ASELLINA

...his is a shop of great interest be...ause it still preserves intact its ...unters and amphorae for the pouring out of drinks. The Thermopolion was in fact the equivalent of a modern bar. The one at Pompeii is really exceptional for the number of its surviving furnishings. The names of some women written on the walls and the presence of some cubicles on the upper floor suggest that the customers of the house were offered the attractions of girls as well as drink.

This is followed by other houses which severally served as **Weavers' Workshops** (characterized by a long balcony), a **Stall for the sale of their wares, a shop** for fruit and vegetables, and then the **HOUSE OF THE INDIAN STATUETTE,** so called because an ivory statuette of Indian provenance was found in it. This is followed by another **THERMOPOLION,** noteworthy for its surviving furnishings and counter, and for its finely decorated Lararium (shrine for the tutelary gods).

Next we come to the **HOUSE OF JULIUS POLYBIUS** (to the left at n° 1-3).

It dates to the Samnite period, but was reconstructed in Roman times. A poem in Latin lamenting the mutability of human affairs is inscribed on one of its walls.

At n° 5 is the **HOUSE OF FABIUS ULULITREMULUS** with its façade decorated with a sq⟍re-panelled

---

Thermopolion of Asellina: view of the counter which held the amphorae for serving drinks.

design in various colours. Frescoes depicting "Aeneas and Anchises" and "Romulus" decorate one wall of its entrance.

Next is the **HOUSE OF THE IMPLUVIUM** (n° 1), with a wonderful **impluvium** decorated with mosaics and inlaid marbles. We then come to the **HOUSE OF SUCCESSUS** (n° 3), so called on account of the inscription placed above a charming painting depicting "A child with a fluttering duck". Next, at n° 5 on the right, we come to

THE HOUSE OF THE ORCHARD

(Casa del Frutteto)
It derives its name from the subjects of the decoration of its cubicles: their walls are completely covered with a fine series of paintings representing many species of fruit trees.We continue our way along the Via dell'Abbondanza, passing on either side the remains of ancient buildings. This brings us, on the left, to

THE HOUSE OF TREBIUS VALENS

(ins. 2, n° 1)

Whose façade bears numerous inscriptions, including announcements of theatrical performances in Pompeii. Particularly noteworthy is the area of its peristyle, whose walls are decorated with a polychrome checkerboard pattern. There is also a charming **triclinium** with water-jetting fountains and one or two rooms with fine paintings.

Just beyond it on the same side of the street is

THE SCHOLA ARMATURARUM

(ins. 3, n° 6)

A building consisting of a huge hall with decorations of military character. It was probably the meeting place of soldiers or of a military association. Next to it is

THE HOUSE OF PINARIUS CERIALIS

Small in size, but very graceful i structure. A hoard of precious gem was found in this house, a fact test fying to the profession of the mas ter of the house, who was probabl not only a seller of precious ob jects, but also a stone-cutter.

A beautiful painting with theatrica scenes may be admired in one o its rooms.

The Via dell'Abbondanza the leads to

THE HOUSE OF THE MORALIST

(On the left at n° 2-3). So called be cause the walls of its **triclinium** (dining room) are depicted with ac monitory verse inscriptions urgin good manners at table; due hosp tality to guests; the avoidance c lascivious glances at other men women; and abstinence from th use of improper or bad-tempere

House of Loreius Tiburtinus.

nguage.

ie house results from the combi-
ation of two intercommunicating
wellings. The first of these is
oteworthy for the decorations
gainst a yellow and black ground
two of its rooms.

st beyond it on the right is

HE HOUSE OF LOREIUS
IBURTINUS (ins. 2, n° 5)

richly decorated, patrician resi-
ence which is among the finest in
ompeii. One enters through a well-
reserved portal which leads into
ie extensive area of the atrium;
iis has a marble **impluvium** at its
entre and is flanked by a series of
oms painted with murals on dif-
rently coloured grounds. Beyond
ie atrium is a long arcaded loggia
great scenic effect: from here the
eries of columns, the pergola, the
ifferent architectural levels and
ie ornamental water-works com-

bine to create a uniquely suggestive environment. The series of
rooms laid out in this area of the
house are, moreover, of considerable interest: all of them are decorated with great refinement and
particularly luxurious.

The **triclinium** is frescoed with wall
paintings representing "Scenes
from the Iliad", all of them distinguished in execution.

Another room is noteworthy for its
wonderful decoration against a
white ground in which, *inter alia*, the
figure of a priest of the cult of Isis,
probably Loreius Tiburtinus himself, may be identified. The garden
is huge in size, and various "casts"
of trees may be seen. Continuing
further along the right of the Via
dell'Abbondanza we come to

THE HOUSE OF VENUS (ins. 3, n° 3)

It is characterized by, and takes its
name from, the large painting of

"Venus on a shell escorted by Cupids" that decorates the end wall of
the garden. To its side is the figure
of "Mars". Other paintings in the
house are either incomplete or
damaged, but a room flanking the
atrium does preserve its fine decoration on a black ground with a "still
life" and "Head of a young lyre-
player".

We now come - again on the right -
to

THE VILLA OF JULIA FELIX (ins. 4, n° 3)

A huge residence which occupies
the whole of one insula in Pompeii.
It consists of three separate sectors:
1) The living quarters: large and
sumptuous, they were once decorated with paintings and statues of
great importance, including the
painting with the group of the "Nine
Muses" now in the Louvre in Paris,
and the terracotta sculpture representing "Pittacos". It was due to the

ouse of **Venus** *- the garden.*

beauty and extensiveness of its rooms that this house has come to be commonly considered a villa. It has a wonderful garden with fish pond, bridges, niches and columns in marble and stucco. The **triclinium** with marble couches is also of interest.

2) The bath-house: this is a large and complete private bath complex which was later rented out as a public baths (as may be read in the notice of location situated beside the entrance). It comprised a vestibule or waiting-room with chairs for the clients, a dressing room, a **frigidarium**, **tepidarium** and **calidarium, a** room for steam baths, and a small open-air pool.

3) Inns and shops: all these premises were rented out by the mistress of the villa. The Via dell'Abbondanza ends with

THE PORTA DI SARNO

This single-arched city gateway is now completely denuded of the tufa facing that once characterized it. It dates to the Samnite period.

Before going through the gate, we turn into the street to the right. This leads to the Piazza dell'Anfiteatro. In this square is situated

THE LARGE PALAESTRA

A huge rectangular area (measuring over 100 metres along each side) designed for gymnastic exercises. It was laid out under the emperor Augustus, since the Small Palaestra close to the Forum had by now become quite inadequate in size.

A perimeter wall runs right round it. Inside, it is arcaded on three sides, the porticoes being pierced by 10 entrances. A large pool is situated at its centre. Close by is the large

AMPHITHEATRE

A wonderful and monumental example of buildings of this kind, it also one of the most ancient know to us. It could accommodate up 12,000 spectators. It had two princ pal entrances and others of less importance. Another passage-w was perhaps reserved for the civ authorities and led directly to the seats.

This amphitheatre has no und ground chambers, perhaps becau combat against wild beasts had n yet become widespread at the tim of its construction, and there w thus no need to provide speci passages and cages for animals.

The Amphitheatre was divided i side into three different series seats. The lowest section of th tiered seats, the so-called **im cavea**, was reserved for people

Villa of Julia Felix.

erial view of the Amphitheatre.
arge Palaestra.

high rank; the middle tiers for the people; and the upper galleries for women. In the topmost part of the Amphitheatre are still visible the large stone rings to which the **velarium** was attached: this was the awning which protected the spectators either from the rain or the sun. The passages leading into the various sectors and the various levels of tiers were provided with a series of stairs.

Making a detour from the Via dell'Abbondanza and turning right into the Via di Porta Nocera (between the 1st and 2nd Region), we may traverse an area which in large part still remains to be excavated. It is, however, of considerable importance for the study of the town, since the complex of houses that have so far been found here testify to the structure and typology of a suburban area. Here we find houses, shops, farmsteads with stables and market gardens: a suburban

world that rounds out our picture of the more demotic side of Pompeii and at the same time throws valuable light on the way of life, the livelihoods and habits of another social class.

Here, for instance, we see the **Thermopolion of the Phoenix, a** kind of open-air bar protected by a pergola; the **Workshop of the Garum,** which was a shop in which a famous sauce was manufactured; and the **House of the Lararium of Sarnus** which was perhaps the house of a fruit-and-vegetable merchant, as would seem to be testified by the painting of the Lararium depicting a "Ship bearing a cargo of the products of the earth".

Continuing in the direction of the Porta Nocera, we come to the **Garden of the Fugitives:** the portico that formed part of a rustic house and its annexed garden in which the bodies of many people who had vainly attempted to flee from

the eruption of Vesuvius wer found. The "casts" made of thes unfortunate victims, heaped t(gether as they fell, their bodie contorted in agony, bear tragic wi ness to that terrible catastrophe.

We come, lastly, to the **Porta N(cera,** another of the gates in Pon peii's circuit of walls, and, beyon it,

THE NECROPOLIS OF PORTA NOCERA

which occupies a vast, and in larg part excavated, area extendin from west to east. In the wester part we may note in particular th large **Tomb of Eumachia** and, to it sides, two aedicula-shaped tomb This is followed by the tombs of th Tillia family, of a freedman, and c the banker Serapion.

Towards the east of the cemeter we find the tomb of the tribune Ce lius, the Mausoleum of Vei Barchilla and a number of altars.

Opposite: The bodies found in the Garden of the Fugitives, a dramatic proof of the tragedy which struck Pompeii wit the eruption of Vesuvius.
Tombs of Porta Nocera: the necropolis extends for along way beyond the perimeter of the city walls.